REACHING THROUGH *the veil*

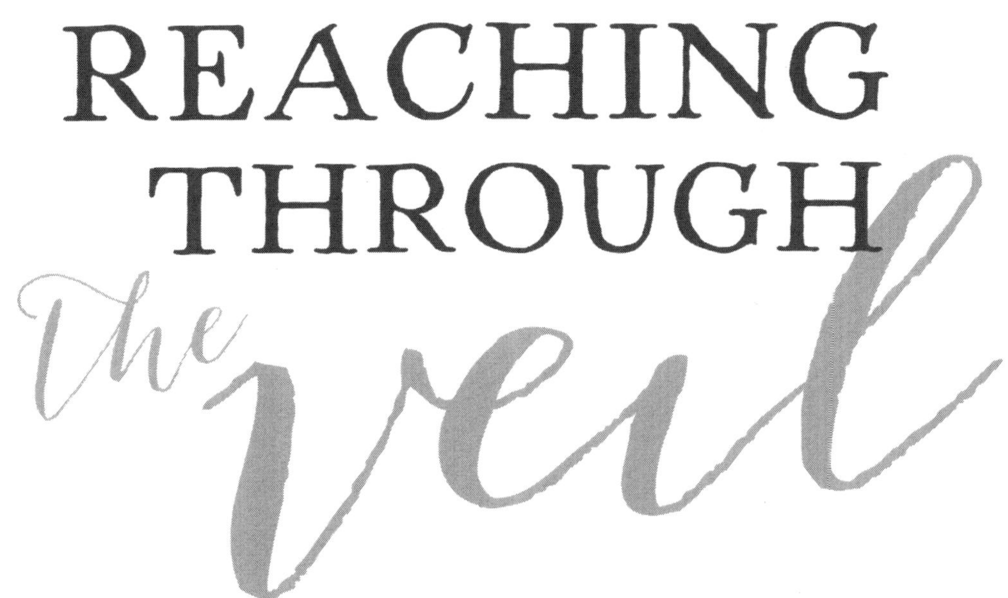

REACHING THROUGH *the veil*

ANGELS IN EVERYDAY LIFE

SHERRIE ANTHONY

CFI
An Imprint of Cedar Fort, Inc.
Springville, Utah

This is not an official publication of The Church of Jesus Christ of Latter-day Saints. The opinions and views expressed herein belong solely to the author and do not necessarily represent the opinions or views of Cedar Fort, Inc. Permission for the use of sources, graphics, and photos is also solely the responsibility of the author.

ISBN 13: 978-1-4621-1871-7

Published by CFI, an imprint of Cedar Fort, Inc.
2373 W. 700 S., Springville, UT 84663
Distributed by Cedar Fort, Inc., www.cedarfort.com

LIBRARY OF CONGRESS CATALOGING-IN-PUBLICATION DATA

Names: Anthony, Sherrie Lyn, 1953- author.
Title: Reaching through the veil / Sherrie Lyn Anthony.
Description: Springville, Utah : CFI, an imprint of Cedar Fort, Inc., [2016]
| Includes bibliographical references and index.
Identifiers: LCCN 2016008156 (print) | LCCN 2016009729 (ebook) | ISBN
9781462118717 (perfect bound : alk. paper) | ISBN 9781462126620 (epub,
pdf, mobi)
Subjects: LCSH: Angels—Church of Jesus Christ of Latter-day Saints. |
Angels—Mormon Church. | Church of Jesus Christ of Latter-day
Saints—Doctrines. | Mormon Church—Doctrines.
Classification: LCC BT966.3 .A58 2016 (print) | LCC BT966.3 (ebook) | DDC
235/.3—dc23
LC record available at http://lccn.loc.gov/2016008156

Cover design by Shawnda T. Craig

Edited and typeset by Deborah Spencer

Printed in the United States of America

10 9 8 7 6 5 4 3 2 1

Printed on acid-free paper

To the littlest angel, Adam Gabriel Prestwich.

Contents

Acknowledgments

A project like this isn't accomplished without help and encouragement. To all my family and friends who read and reread this book, thank you. To Arthur McKinlay, who spent hours tutoring, correcting, and transforming a brain dump into a manuscript, I thank him. He is truly an angel of mercy who never lost faith in the project. To David Anthony, my friend, my support, and my husband, I owe my deepest appreciation. He wouldn't let me quit and I am indebted to him for his assistance, his proofing skills, and his encouragement. And a special thank you to that little angel, Gabriel Prestwich, who opened my eyes to the glorious help that rests on the other side of the veil.

Introduction

On September 11, 2008, I started to study the role and impact of angels in our lives. This was initiated by a very sacred experience that occurred in our family. My study continued when I was asked to speak at several firesides. The more I studied, the more I realized that I was unaware of angels in the gospel plan, and from the comments I received after the firesides, I realized that many others were uninformed as well. The reason I chose to write this book was to enlighten or remind us of the heavenly help that angels offer.

One of the ways the Lord communicates with man is through angels. The Lord, "knowing all things. . .sent angels to minister unto the children of men" (Moroni 7:22). Angels are not the only way God communicates with us, but they are one of the ways. We need to remember that "there were divers ways that he [the Lord] did manifest things unto the children of men" (Moroni 7:24). Inspiration from the Lord comes primarily through the Holy Ghost, but we can receive direction from the light of Christ, the Lord Himself, prophets and apostles, inspired associates, the scriptures, and, as this book will show, angels.

These various ways of receiving messages from the Lord may be difficult to distinguish between. What we are sure of is that "all things which are good cometh of Christ" (Moroni 7:24). What I would like to emphasize is that we should not discount that angels are ministering to us, but recognize the possibility that inspiration could and does come from angels.

Our Angel Gabe

This book was inspired by an angel that came into our lives on September 11, 2008. Precious Adam Gabriel Prestwich—Gabe—only drew breath for 2 hours and 17 minutes, but he changed the lives of everyone that knew him.

My daughter, Lisa, was excited as the day drew closer for her to find out if she was going to have a girl or a boy. I will let Gabe's mother, Lisa, tell his story:

It mattered to Gabe . . .

> "I'm so sorry to tell you this but there is a problem with your baby." These words seemed to echo in my mind.
>
> What was supposed to be a routine ultrasound at four months of pregnancy suddenly turned into a nightmare. I was scheduled immediately to meet with a perinatologist. Completely overwhelmed, I kept telling myself that it would be okay. We had two healthy boys, ages three and four, and this was probably a misunderstanding.
>
> The doctor went over the ultrasound carefully and with tears in his eyes tried to explain that our child had a rare condition called anencephaly. Although the baby looked healthy and his heart was perfect, his head had not formed correctly and he would not be born with more than a brain stem. The doctor continued to explain that the probability of carrying this baby to full term was rare, the baby most likely would not survive birth, and if he did survive he would likely only live for minutes.

A counselor was sent to go into more detail about the situation and our options. I could choose not to see the baby at all and the hospital would take care of the remains or I could see the baby and we could take care of the body. The counselor said, "I am very familiar with the prominent religions in this area." (Being from Salt Lake City, it was obvious he was talking about The Church of Jesus Christ of Latter-day Saints.) He continued, 'none of the religions would have any problem with you being induced now and ending the pregnancy.' He explained that there could be complications for me and the outcome for our baby would be the same no matter what we did. Our baby would die.

This news was more than I could process or deal with and I just wanted everything to go away. As I walked out of the hospital, I saw a mother with her new baby being carefully loaded into their car for their first trip home. It was almost more than I could bear.

On the car ride home my husband and I decided we would contact our bishop to talk to him about the situation and get the final go ahead with being induced early.

When we sat down with our bishop and explained the situation, I was surprised to hear his counsel. Our bishop explained that he and his wife had wanted more children but had not been able to have more. He said that even if this child was not with us here on earth he would still be our son and we would have him for eternity.

Immediately we knew what we needed to do. We wanted this child to be part of our family for as long as possible. Although the pain and sadness continued over the weeks, it was slowly replaced with peace and hope. I found joy in picking out the perfect outfit for him to wear and the little mementos I wanted to remember him by.

The weeks carried on and some of the complications began to manifest as I struggled physically to carry this child. Although physically each day got harder, spiritually I found myself growing closer to the amazing child that was part of our eternal family.

At 37 weeks of pregnancy, I was put on bed rest. After spending a week in bed due to complications from the pregnancy, I went back to see the doctor to make sure that I wasn't progressing too quickly and that Gabe (our baby) was doing okay. Earlier in the week they had found some sort of infection and had put me on antibiotics and Gabe's heartbeat was 30 beats slower per minute than it should have been. After the doctor checked me he said that he would be very surprised if I made it past the weekend without delivering the baby.

I got up the next morning determined to get the cleaning done.

As I cleaned, Gabe (who was a very active baby) was kicking and wiggling in my womb. I talked to him as I cleaned, hoping he would be able to recognize my voice after he was born.

I was nearly done cleaning and was probably in the least attractive room in the house (the unfinished laundry room) when I suddenly felt the Spirit come over me so strongly that I couldn't deny its presence. I felt such an overwhelming concern and worry that I put down the broom and I asked, "What's wrong, Gabe?" (Looking back, or thinking about what was about to happen, I would have thought it shocking or amazing, but what happened next was so natural and normal that it didn't faze me in the least.) As I waited for the answer, I felt this sweet child begin to move in my womb at the same time I heard him say, "I'm scared."

I said, "What are you scared of?"

He said, "I'm scared it's going to hurt."

I knew he was talking about the delivery. I told him that I too was afraid of the delivery. It was going to be hard for both of us, but I would be there and together we would get through it. I pleaded with him to stay strong and not to give up, it would be hard but we wanted so much to be with him. I began telling him about his dad. I told him how much his dad wanted to meet him and how much he loved him. I told him how big his dad's hands are (Adam is 6 feet 4 inches and weighs 250 pounds) and that they are always warm. I told him he would know his dad immediately and that he would feel his love for him. I told Gabe it was necessary that we both be strong, because it was very important to his brothers that they get to meet him. Once again my womb began to move and I heard him answer, "It is important to me too. I want to be with them. I want to play all the games they play." Hearing Gabe say this, two things came to my mind: 1) he really did know and love his brothers and 2) I realized his true desire to be with them and us eternally.

Gabe then said to me, "Don't forget me." I almost laughed at the thought of it being possible for us to forget him. I reassured him, "Gabe, we will never forget you." Once again he said, "Please don't forget me." Again I said, "Gabe, you are so important to us, we will never forget you, you are part of our family." A third time he said, "No, don't forget me. Don't forget where I am. Don't forget that I am waiting for you. Don't forget how much I want to be with you again." I was shocked, realizing what Gabe was saying to me. He was concerned about us and our eternal salvation and our goal as a family. Of course this has always been our goal, to be an eternal family, but I saw that it was vital that we achieve this goal or we would not be with this child who was determined to be with us.

I cried as I tried to comfort Gabe and tell him that we would do all in our power to live the way we should and do the things we should so that we would be together again. I felt, and know, that he understood the difficulties we face here on earth; he knew we had a veil over our eyes which could cause us to lose sight of what our true goal is in this life. I also felt, saw, and heard in his voice that there was not a veil over his eyes and he knew without a doubt what our mission was in the eternal plan.

I told Gabe how important he is to us and how thankful I am to be his mother. He said, "I really want to be with my brothers and my family, but I chose to follow this path and I want to do this." Once again I knew he had perfect sight of the plan of salvation and there were only two things that were truly important: 1) Heavenly Father and Jesus Christ and 2) our eternal family. I sensed that even though he had chosen this path, he knew it would lead to greater good. He needed this body to progress in the plan. Gabe fully understood the plan of our Father in Heaven. He had chosen this path and he was happy, excited, and completely willing to be an instrument in the Savior's hands to further the work. Yet, he felt sadness because he had to sacrifice his earthly time with us. Still, he knew where he was needed at this time. I told him that his brothers would need his help in their lives. He said, "I know, and I will be with them." I said, "Your dad and I are going to need your help and guidance." He said, "I know, and I will need your help."

His answer surprised me because I didn't think that he would need us once he was gone. Thinking back I can understand ways that we can help our dear child accomplish his current mission, such as doing family history research, but I don't know if there will be more for us to do. I told Gabe that Adam and I would do all we could to stay close to the Spirit and be receptive to his needs. At this point I felt some of the concern begin to ease. I walked in and sat on the couch, and I cried as I told my sweet baby how much I loved him. For that moment, in some sort of spiritual way, he was nestled in my arms and I could feel him snuggle into me like only a baby does with his mother.

Within a few minutes our two boys, Avram and Briggs, came running downstairs like a hurricane. When they found me I told them to sing a song for Gabe. They chose to sing "Itsy Bitsy Spider."

Gabe wiggled and squirmed in my womb with delight and joy hearing his brothers and feeling like part of the pack.

I left this experience knowing how much Gabe loves us, how perfect his sight is without being blocked by the veil and how much he loves the Savior.

Exactly one week later, Gabe was born and lived for 2 hours and 17 minutes. He fought for every breath of air he took. He lived for his family and he delighted in the few minutes he spent with each one of us. His father, assisted by my father, tenderly gave him a name and a blessing—Adam Gabriel Prestwich. He slipped away peacefully being comforted by the love and warmth that radiated from his father's hands.

Shortly after his death, I hemorrhaged and lost consciousness. It took hours before I was stable once again. I turned to my mother, who had been sitting by my bedside for hours, and I said, "I thought it would be years before I could say this, but I'm thankful I carried this child and that I was able to go through this experience."

We had been told several months earlier that it wouldn't matter if we carried the baby full term or induced labor early. I testify that it mattered. This child lived and changed the lives of many people. He has given me hope, joy, and a determination to keep our goal to be an eternal family. We were able to donate his heart valves in hopes of helping someone else. His strength and love has given so many people and myself a greater understanding of the spirits that anxiously await their turn for a body and to be part of our Father in Heaven's plan.

I still long for my child, but I am thankful for the inspired counsel we received and followed. I am thankful for the knowledge of the plan of happiness and the Atonement, which makes it possible.

You can imagine the comfort this experience brought to Lisa and Adam and those that loved them. This marked the beginning of my study about angels. This little angel, Gabe, is the inspiration behind this book. When Lisa and Adam gave me permission to share Gabe's story, it was with the hope that someone's life would be blessed by his short tenure on earth. Perhaps his story could bring hope and faith in Christ to others that faced similar situations.

Gabe helped me to see that the veil between this world and the world of spirits is very thin. He taught me that there are spirits on the other side of the veil that love us and are concerned about our welfare. He showed me that God has a plan for each of us and as the Apostle Paul stated "It is a fearful thing to fall into the hands of the living God" (Hebrews 10:31), but when we submit to the Lord's will, great things can happen. Gabe helped me refocus some of my priorities.

I have come to believe that our tragedies can be turned into blessings if we love the Lord. "And we know that all things work together for good to them that love God" (Romans 8:28). When the storms of life pass, there is a rainbow waiting at the other end that helps make sense of the hailstorm.

The Provo Tabernacle has taught this very concept. Linda S. Reeves, second counselor in the Relief Society general presidency taught this principle to the sisters at the general Relief Society meeting on September 28, 2013.

> Almost three years ago a devastating fire gutted the interior of the beloved, historic tabernacle in Provo, Utah. Its loss was deemed a great tragedy by both the community and Church members. Many wondered, "Why did the Lord let this happen? Surely He could have prevented the fire or stopped its destruction."
>
> Ten months later, during the October 2011 general conference, there was an audible gasp when President Thomas S. Monson announced that the nearly destroyed tabernacle was to become a holy temple—a house of the Lord! Suddenly we could see what the Lord had always known! He didn't cause the fire, but He allowed the fire to strip away the interior. He saw the tabernacle as a magnificent temple—a permanent home for making sacred, eternal covenants.. . .
>
> The trials and tribulation that we experience may be the very things that guide us to come unto Him and cling to our covenants so that we might return to His presence and receive all that the Father hath.[1]

Just as Gabe's short life appeared to be a tragedy, other misfortunes may at first appear to be devastating, when in reality the Lord knows far more than our mortal comprehension can understand. He may be orchestrating the building of a sanctified soul.

Our little angel, Gabe, gave us the pearl we could cling to. As my daughter said, "Gabe fully understood the plan of our Father in Heaven. He had chosen this path and he was happy, excited, and completely willing to be an instrument in the Savior's hands to further the work." May we likewise be an instrument for good in the Savior's hands.

Who Are the Angels?

The term angel means 'messenger.' An angel is any messenger sent by God to do His work."[2]

The Bible Dictionary divides angels into two groups, those with bodies and those without bodies (see Bible Dictionary, "Angels"):

Angels with bodies of flesh and bone are resurrected or translated beings.

Angels that appeared to Joseph Smith at the beginning of the restoration to instruct him and give him the keys of the priesthood were both resurrected and translated beings with bodies of flesh and bone. Moroni, John the Baptist, Peter, James, Elijah, and other resurrected beings appeared to Joseph and restored keys and knowledge vital for the Restoration of the gospel.

There was a key figure in the Restoration that was a translated being, John the Beloved. He appeared with Peter and James to restore the Melchizedek Priesthood. During the Savior's mortal ministry, John the Beloved asked the Savior to be allowed the opportunity to remain on the earth until the Savior returned. The scriptures explain the state of translated beings in 3 Nephi 28 when the three Nephite Apostles also requested to remain on the earth until the Savior returned.

John the Beloved was assigned to be a ministering angel. "I will make him as flaming fire and a *ministering angel*; he shall minister for those who shall be heirs of salvation who dwell on the earth" (D&C 7:6; emphasis added).

The City of Enoch, which was translated, was given the assignment to be ministering angels as well. Orson Pratt of the Quorum of the Twelve Apostles taught, "They [i.e., Enoch and his people] have been gone, as I have already stated, about five thousand years. What have they been doing? All that we know concerning this subject is what has been revealed through the great and mighty Prophet of the last days, Joseph Smith—that unlearned youth whom God raised up to bring forth the Book of Mormon and to establish this latter-day Church. He has told us *that they have been ministering angels during all that time.*"[3]

The Three Nephites fulfilled the mission of ministering angels to Mormon. In the scriptures, Mormon declared, "Behold, I have seen them, and they have ministered unto me" (3 Nephi 28:26). Moroni also confirmed the fact that they were ministered to by the Three Nephites. "My father and I have seen them, and they have ministered unto us" (Mormon 8:11). These faithful men surrounded by wickedness were ministered to and strengthened by angels.

A story is told about John the Beloved (also known as John the Revelator) visiting the Prophet Joseph Smith and warning him to immediately return to Nauvoo. Allen Stout served as a bodyguard to Joseph and told this story to Martha C. Cox. She related the story:

> He [Allen Stout] was once walking with the Prophet on the west side of the Mississippi River on the road to Montrose, I think. They saw a man walking along a road leading in from the south and coming towards them. The Prophet told Allen to remain where he was while he stepped over to speak with this pedestrian. Allen turned his back towards them and for a time forgot the Prophet and became engaged with his own thoughts, while he stood whipping a low bush with the cane he carried. The hand of the Prophet upon his shoulder aroused him. The Prophet said, "We must return immediately to Nauvoo." They walked silently and rapidly. Allen became very sorrowful over his recreancy to his duty and could not refrain from weeping. The prophet asked him why he wept. Allen confessed, "I am an insufficient bodyguard—criminally neglectful of your welfare. I allowed that man you met to speak with you without even being ready to

> defend if he attacked you. He could have killed you and made his escape without my knowing who he is, which way he went or what he even looks like. You will have to dispense with my services and take a guard on which you can depend. Your life is too precious to be trusted to my care." The Prophet then said, "that man would not harm me. You saw John the Revelator."[4]

Allen could not describe the angel or where he went. But he was aware of the personage. John the Revelator had been sent to Joseph, not Allen.

There was no one resurrected until Jesus Christ was resurrected. The Apostle Paul explained it this way, "But now is Christ risen from the dead, and become the first fruits of them that slept" (1 Corinthians 15:20). Abinadi in the Book of Mormon confirmed that truth, "And if Christ had not risen from the dead, or have broken the bands of death that the grave should have no victory, and that death should have no sting, there could have been no resurrection" (Mosiah 16:7). Therefore, angels before Christ's resurrection were of three forms. The first form is translated beings. Second is unembodied spirits, which are angels from the premortal world who had not yet obtained a body. Finally, disembodied spirits are those who have lived on this earth and died and dwell in the spirit world and are waiting for the resurrection.

There were prophets translated in the Old Testament so they could pass on priesthood keys to Peter, James, and John on the Mount of Transfiguration during the Savior's ministry. "Translated beings are assigned special ministries . . . as in the case of Moses and Elijah, who were translated in order to appear with physical bodies hundreds of years later on the mount of transfiguration prior to the resurrection of Christ. Had they been spirits only, they could not have laid hands on the mortal Peter, James, and John (D&C 129:3–8)."[5]

Angels are spirits from either the premortal world or spirits from the spirit world waiting for the resurrection.

The Savior's appearance to the brother of Jared in the Book of Mormon is an example of an unembodied spirit from the premortal world. The brother of Jared had gone to the mountain to plead with the Lord to touch the stones he had molted out of the mountain to enable the Jaredites to have light as they crossed the ocean to the promised land. When the brother of Jared saw the finger of the Lord, he exclaimed, "I knew not that the Lord had flesh and blood" (Ether 3:8).

Then the Savior explained, "Behold, this body, which ye now behold, is the body of my spirit; and man have I created after the body of my spirit; and even as I appear unto thee to be in the spirit will I appear unto my people in the flesh" (Ether 3:16).

While the Savior's body lay in the tomb after the crucifixion, his disembodied spirit went to the spirit world. Joseph Smith said, "Jesus Christ became a ministering spirit (while His body was lying in the sepulcher) to the spirits in prison."[6]

Spirits that come from the premortal world are adult spirits and are born into infant bodies.

President Joseph F. Smith teaches,

> The spirits of our children are immortal before they come to us, and their spirits, after bodily death, are like they were before they came. They are as they would have appeared if they had lived in the flesh, to grow to maturity, or to develop their physical bodies to the full stature of their spirits. If you see one of your children that has passed away it may appear to you in the form in which you would recognize it, the form of childhood; but if it came to you as a messenger bearing some important truth, it would perhaps come as the spirit of Bishop Edward Hunter's son (who died when a little child) came to him, in the stature of full-grown manhood, and revealed himself to his father, and said: I am your son."[7]

I bring this point up because when Gabe talked to his mother he talked and reasoned with her as an adult would because he was an adult spirit. If you lose a child and that child were to come to you as a ministering angel, it might appear in the form you would recognize, but he or she would be an adult spirit.

As the extended family was preparing for the heartache we would all suffer when Gabe was born, our family was hit by another heart rendering tragedy. August 13, 2008—four weeks before

Gabe was born—my nephew, Jaron, and niece, Michelle, lost their 14-month-old son, Gavin. Gavin's death left an irreplaceable hole in the family. They were living with my elder brother, Jeff, and my sister-in-law Karen at the time when my niece put Gavin down for the night. She returned twenty minutes later to check on him and he was not breathing. She was trained in infant CPR and started immediately. My nephew and brother gave him a blessing as 911 was called. Gavin was a perfectly healthy baby, so his death was labeled sudden infant death syndrome, SIDS. SIDS usually occurs before the age of one and has no explanation. His death left the family shocked that God had taken him back. There was no other reason why he should have died. The following experience of my brother's occurred while he was in the hospital after Gavin had passed away. Jeff shared this experience with me on November 1, 2008.

"Gavin had already passed away. We were in the emergency room for a while. The doctor said they had worked on him but there was no response. It had been an hour since Gavin passed away. His mother asked if she could hold him for a while. They said yes, 'let's have you go to another room and you can hold him as long as you want'.

"We went into a separate room were Michelle held Gavin. It was quiet in the room. Once in a while someone would come in and out. Karen and the bishop came in and out of the room several times. Other than that I am not sure there was anyone else in the room besides Michelle and me. I was sitting there feeling down and so distraught over what had happened. I had my head down. Something either startled me or got my attention or something caused me to look up. I saw Gavin. He didn't see me. It is almost as though I had been walking down a hall and crossed an intersecting hall. I looked down and saw someone standing there. I only saw him for maybe a second. I saw him well enough that I knew it was him. I could recognize him if I passed him on the street. I could describe him. He was tall and thin and had light-colored hair. He looked very similar to his father, Jaron, only a little bit taller. He appeared to be in a conversation talking to someone else. He seemed to be in an intense conversation with whomever the person was. I didn't see who he was talking to but it seemed to be important. I remember him being kind of distinguished looking and you have that feeling in a split second that this is an important person. This is all an impression as I did not see him with my eyes. The way I can describe it is that I felt an image. It happened very quickly and it was over and gone.

"When it happened I looked around to see if I could see anything else. I looked up to see if he was really there. He was not there. It happened all so quick and indescribable that for a while I wasn't sure that I had seen what I thought I saw. But I knew it was Gavin and he was an adult. It was distinct enough that I could pick him out of a group of a thousand people."

Despite this experience, Gavin's mother could not find peace. Gavin is still missed and always be, but his mother has since had experiences that have brought her comfort. One day Gavin's mother blogged the following experience, which reminds us that our loved ones are aware of us and watching.

August 12, 2009

> This happened about 2 weeks ago. I didn't get a chance to write it down. And don't ask me why but for some reason, it seems easier to express my thoughts and feelings in writing than aloud. I am sure that some of my family members will read this and wonder why I didn't share this personally with them. I guess writing here is easier for me to get my thoughts out, or there's never the right time or place to share a story like this. I guess sometimes there are no "right words" to describe it. I hope this makes sense.
>
> I was downstairs with Sawyer, [her second son], sitting in my rocking chair. He was starting to fuss a little bit, I started to sing to him. I've avoided singing any of the primary songs that I sang to Gavin. I just haven't been ready. I started to sing the Primary song "Love is Spoken Here."
>
> . . . As I sang the words "her plea to the Father quiets all my fears," I felt a thought. My mind was impressed with the feeling, "Yes, Mom, your pleas, your prayers to the Father, quiets my fears, it strengthens me to hear your words, to hear your faith." At which point I started to cry. The thought came suddenly to my mind, from nowhere. It was as though someone spoke the words to me, but it was the feeling I felt. I thought that it must be Gavin. I continued

> the song, "And I am thankful, love is spoken here" and the feelings continued in my mind. "Mama, I am thankful love is spoken here. I am grateful that you love my Dad, and that my Dad returns that love to you. I watch and see it between you both and my brother. And I AM THANKFUL. LOVE. IS. SPOKEN. HERE." The experience is hard to describe, because it was an exchange between spirits. I didn't hear the words. I felt them. And they weren't words that I felt, but rather feelings that were kind of like words. I struggle to find the right WORDS to describe this. But it was love that I felt. And it was precious. Oh, how I love my little Gavibear. Thank you my sweet boy. Mama needed that.

There is one more classification of angels: We can be ministering angels!

There are the immortal angels that are ministering to man as well as mortal angels.

Elder Jeffrey R. Holland testified of different kinds of angels: "On occasions, global or personal, we may feel we are distanced from God, shut out from heaven, lost, alone in dark and dreary places. Often enough that distress can be of our own making, but even then the Father of us all is watching and assisting. And always there are those angels *who come and go all around us, seen and unseen, known and unknown, mortal and immortal*."[8]

Our angels that come to rescue us do not need to come from another province. They can live right next door to us. "The term angel means 'messenger.' An angel is *any* messenger sent by God to do *His* work."[9] Therefore if we are on an errand for the Lord, we are serving as an angel. The Lord often uses mortal angels to answer our prayers. President Spencer W. Kimball told us why serving each other is so important: "God does notice us, and he watches over us. But it is usually through another person that he meets our needs. Therefore, it is vital that we serve each other in the kingdom."[10]

President Thomas S. Monson is an ideal example of serving others. He has mastered the ability to listen to the promptings from the Lord and to be a messenger of God. He said, "The sweetest experience I know in life is to feel a prompting and act upon it and later find out that it was the fulfillment of someone's prayer or someone's need. And I always want the Lord to know that if He needs an errand run, Tom Monson will run that errand for Him"[11]

As we serve and follow the promptings we are given, we too can literally run errands for the Lord. What a privilege to serve our Lord in that manner.

President Thomas S. Monson told the story of a woman who acted as an angel to a sister she hardly knew. Tiffany was a young mother who became overwhelmed by the demands of her situation. Her husband was in medical residency and not able to help with the family and the demands of four children. The holiday season arrived, and they had extra holiday guests that put an extra burden on Tiffany. To add to the mounting pressure, Tiffany's friend was diagnosed with cancer. Tiffany slipped into a period of depression, losing weight and sinking deeper and deeper into despair. She felt abandoned by the Lord; all her efforts to find peace and help were unsuccessful. Her friends tried to get her to eat, but no matter what they brought to her she could only eat a bite or two. Finally, in an attempt to get Tiffany to eat something, Tiffany's friend asked what sounded good to her. Tiffany thought and responded, "Homemade bread." But there was no homemade bread available. But the Lord was aware of her needs and had a plan in place. The angel's name was Sherrie. She had met Tiffany at Thanksgiving when Tiffany was visiting her sister, Nicole. You can imagine then the surprise on Tiffany's husband face when the doorbell rang and Sherrie, nearly a complete stranger, was standing there with a loaf of homemade bread.

> Tiffany called her sister Nicole to thank her for sending Sherrie on an errand of mercy. Instead, she learned Nicole had not instigated the visit and had no knowledge of it.
>
> The rest of the story unfolded as Nicole checked with her friend Sherrie to find out what had prompted her to deliver that loaf of bread. What she learned was an inspiration to her, to Tiffany, to Sherrie—and it is an inspiration to me.
>
> On that particular morning of the bread delivery, Sherrie had been prompted to make two loaves of bread instead of the one she had planned to make. She said she felt impressed to take the second loaf with her in her car that day, although she didn't know why. After lunch at a friend's home, her one-year-old daughter began to

> cry and needed to be taken home for a nap. Sherrie hesitated when the unmistakable feeling came to her that she needed to deliver that extra loaf of bread to Nicole's sister Tiffany, who lived 30 minutes away on the other side of town and whom she barely knew. She tried to rationalize away the thought, wanting to get her very tired daughter home and feeling sheepish about delivering a loaf of bread to people who were almost strangers. However, the impression to go to Tiffany's home was strong, so she heeded the prompting.
>
> When she arrived, Tiffany's husband answered the door. Sherrie reminded him that she was Nicole's friend whom he'd met briefly at Thanksgiving, handed him the loaf of bread, and left.[12]

Because a very busy young mother listened to the promptings of the spirit, Tiffany received not only the loaf of homemade bread but a message from the Lord that He was aware of her struggles. Sherrie was the angel to answer Tiffany's plea and the instrument in the Lord's hand to show her His love.

Just as Sherrie was sent from the Lord to meet Tiffany's need, the Lord has missionaries throughout the world that act as angels to thousands of Heavenly Father's children daily.

The missionary force of the Church as of April's 2015 general conference was 85,147 full-time missionaries and 30,404 Church service missionaries. Our missionaries fit the definition of angels. These missionaries are not only sent by God but, being set apart to teach His word, they roam through the world serving others and bringing a message of hope and salvation. They are a royal army of angels working for the Lord. In 2005, my daughter served a mission in Madrid, Spain. She served in the capacity of an angel for a complete stranger as she and her companion brought a message of hope and love from the Lord. I was touched by one of her sweet letters home:

> We were stood up by our appointments tonight and decided to go and check on old contacts that we had. As we walked through a park I made eye contact with a woman who was sitting on a bench who looked like she was in her fifties or sixties. She looked like a Spaniard. I had the impression that we needed to talk to her. My first reaction was, "No, I am not in the mood to be rejected right now." The older Spaniard generation is always happy to have someone to talk to but

you never get anywhere with them. They always say, "I was born Catholic and I will die Catholic," and they never listen to anything you say concerning religion.

As we passed her I again had an impression that we needed to talk to her. Once again I said, "No, I really don't want to be turned down right now." We passed her and for some reason I decided that I needed to follow that impression whether anything came of it or not. We went back and introduced ourselves as missionaries for the Church of Jesus Christ of Latter-day Saints and asked if she had a few minutes to listen to a message about the Savior. She said yes. I almost started to walk away because I never get that response and it took me by surprise.

We sat down and the first thing she said to me was, "Many people think I am a Spaniard but I am not. I am from Romania." She went on to tell us about how she came to Spain. Her daughter married a Spaniard who later cheated on her and kicked her daughter out. Her daughter wanted to take her life and so she went to help the daughter. She left a job working at a hospital in Romania to clean homes in Spain and had been here for seven years. At this point she was crying uncontrollably. We sat and listened to her. When she was finished I bore testimony of the Savior and his power to heal and about eternal families.

As we got ready to leave you could see her burden had been lifted. She had a smile on her face and was excited for us to come and teach her more. She gave us her address and committed to come to church the next day. We never saw her again. We went to the address she gave us and we never got an answer at the door. I was so grateful that I had followed the Spirit. I was taught very strongly the importance of following the Holy Ghost when it spoke to me. I was grateful to be an instrument for the Lord to help lift the burdens of one of his children and help them to feel of his love for them.

Our missionaries are messengers of hope to a world that is in commotion. In this next account, missionaries were the angels that a man prayed for.

A young 17-year-old convert working with a newly called full-time missionary saw the Lord use his servant to answer the prayer of a man that had decided to end his life. The full-time missionary ordered his companion and driver for the night to stop the car.

The missionary felt impressed that someone in an uninviting house needed their help. The young convert was not convinced that this was a good idea but the missionary insisted.

> "Elder, I don't think anybody's home. We can try some other time."
>
> "Just wait," the missionary pleaded.
>
> Just as I was about to drag my temporary companion away from the dark doorstep, the door creaked open. In front of us stood a short, skinny man in his mid-30s. He wore a pair of tattered jeans and an off-white T-shirt decorated with small holes and grease stains.
>
> "Who are you?" the man softly inquired.
>
> "I am Elder Johnson, and this is my friend Gabe. We are here on behalf of the Lord Jesus Christ."
>
> Tears began to roll down the man's face, and he started to sob uncontrollably. We stood in front of him, absolutely amazed at the scene that was unfolding before our eyes. Behind the tears he was shedding, the man's eyes lit up with hope.
>
> "Are you the angels I asked for?" the man questioned.
>
> It turns out that Sam, the man we were speaking with, had been planning to end his life that night. In a final prayer to God, he pleaded that he would receive forgiveness for what he was about to do. Finally, his last hopeful request was for the Lord to send him an angel in this time of great need.
>
> A fire burned in my chest as I realized the Lord was using this missionary and me as instruments in His hands. I felt so foolish for doubting the elder's impression to stop.[13]

Our missionary force is truly an army of angels bringing God's love, His message, and His tender mercies to a world in need. Yet, we don't have to be a full-time missionary to have the Lord use us in the very same way.

Starting in 1994, I experienced a very difficult period of time with depression in my life that lasted for several years. Prior to this I had never known depression or a total lack of hope. I was so overcome with sadness that I could no longer feel happiness. I continued to go through the routine of my life but I could not feel joy. I would look out the window and see the sun and wonder if I would ever feel that burst of joy and the love of life again. I could not feel happiness even though good things were happening around me. I visited the temple weekly and tried to function, but my heart and mind were not into the joy of living. I was only surviving. I attended a Relief Society conference that changed my life. Sister Okazaki, who was serving in the Relief Society general presidency, was that heavenly messenger for me.

Sister Okazaki was an angel that spoke by the power of the Holy Ghost. "How could ye speak with the tongue of angels save it were by the Holy Ghost?" (2 Nephi 32:2). That night I received a message from the Lord through this faithful dedicated sister. Sister Okazaki was an angel with a divine message for me. I walked out of that meeting with hope for the first time in many years where despair had been destroying my life. Sister Okazaki said,

> Oh sisters, dearest sisters, choose life even though the forces of death seem strong! Choose hope even though despair seems close! Choose to grow even though circumstances oppress you! Choose to learn even though you must struggle against your own ignorance and that of others! Choose to love, even though ours are days of violence and vengeance. Choose to forgive, to pray, to bless another's life with simple kindness. Choose to build the sisterhood of the Relief Society by lifting and strengthening one another with love, testimony, faith, and service. I promise that you will feel the abundant love of the Savior.[14]

I left that evening saying "I choose hope" even though my situation did not look hopeful. I could not live any longer with despair. In time I found hope because of the message I received from Sister Okazaki. Her message that night was for me, or so I felt.

Elder Jeffrey R. Holland reminded us, "Not all angels are from the other side of the veil. Some of them we walk with and talk with—here, now, every day. Some of them reside in our own neighborhoods. Some of them gave birth to us, and in my case, one of them consented to marry me. Indeed heaven never seems closer than when we see the love God manifested in the kindness and devotion of people so good and so pure that *angelic* is the only word that comes to mind."[15]

How many times in our lives has someone called at the right time or said what we needed to hear or put their arm around us when we needed a hug. Our neighbors, friends, and associates are angels indeed.

From the hymn "As Sisters in Zion," we find the following words: "The errand of angels is given to women. . . . To cheer and to bless in humanity's name."[16]

The sisters of the Relief Society organization are on an errand to lift those around us. The Relief Society motto is "charity never faileth." One of the greatest services a woman can render is that of being a mother. Elder Russell M. Nelson quoted the First Presidency: "Many years ago the First Presidency issued a statement that has had a profound and lasting influence upon me. 'Motherhood,' they wrote, 'is near to divinity. It is the highest, holiest service to be assumed by mankind. It places her who honors its holy calling and service next to the angels.'"[17]

Not only is a mother's service similar to angels' but the Prophet Joseph Smith gave this promise to the women of the Church shortly after he organized the Relief Society. "This is a charitable Society, and according to your natures; it is natural for females to have feelings of charity and benevolence. . . . If you live up to these principles, how great and glorious will be your reward in the celestial kingdom! If you live up to your privileges, the angels *cannot be restrained from being your associates.*"[18]

As we serve our families and those around us, we will have the companionship of angels. We may never know how many times we have been the ministering angel for another. May we not forget that our angelic service may be to our own family members. An account from the *Ensign* demonstrates how our family members serve as angels.

> My husband and I were deeply touched when our daughter, Stephanie, shared the following journal entry with us, written when she was in seventh grade. I share it with her permission:
>
> "One day while we were reading our scriptures, we talked about how important it is for each of us to have our own knowledge and testimony—and that we must not put off asking Heavenly Father for this. That night I went to my room and shut the door. I waited until everything was very quiet. Then I knelt down by my bed and

> prayed. I asked Heavenly Father to please send me an angel to tell me for sure if the gospel was true. He answered that he would, and I was to get in bed and wait for the angel to come. I felt very peaceful and happy, and I waited.
>
> "The house was very still, and I think I had dropped off to sleep. I woke up when I heard a voice. It was Mother. She was kneeling beside my bed praying. She was praying for me. I listened, and when she finished I touched her hair so she would know I was awake. She put her arms around me and held me and her face was wet. She told me I had a Father in Heaven and that he loved me. She said she was glad he had let me come to live in our family. She told me he sent his own Son here to give his life so we could return to live with him if we obeyed his commandments. She told me to always remember that the gospel had been restored, and I must live it so I could go back to my Father.
>
> "We held each other for a while," Stephanie continued, "and then Mother left. After she left, Father in Heaven said to my mind, 'I sent you your angel.' "[19]

We may be sent on an angelic mission by the whispering of an angel. If that service was inspired by an angel, it is very likely we would not be able to distinguish it was an angel. Elder Dallin H. Oaks said, "The ministering of angels can also be unseen. Angelic messages can be delivered by a voice or merely by thoughts or feelings communicated to the mind."[20]

One of the confusing questions that presents itself is, when am I being influenced by an angel or by the Holy Ghost? This is what we know. Angels are agents of the Holy Ghost. Angels speak by the power of the Holy Ghost. President Boyd K. Packer taught, "We are told that 'angels speak by the power of the Holy Ghost.' We are even told that when we speak by the power of the Holy Ghost, we 'speak with the tongue [or in the same language] of angels.' . . . Revelation comes as words we feel more than hear. . . . The Lord reveals His will through dreams and visions, visitations, through angels, through His own voice, and through the voice of His servants. 'Whether by mine own voice,' He said, 'or by the voice of my servants, it is the same.' "[21]

No matter what manner the Lord uses to speak to us, whether it be the Holy Ghost, an angel, the Lord's prophets, inspired church leaders, or a friend, the message is what the Lord would have us know. Joseph Smith taught that there was an order in heaven: "The most perfect order and harmony: their limits and bounds were fixed irrevocably, and voluntarily subscribed to in their heavenly estates."[22] The message delivered to us by angels is the will of the Lord. Angels have limits and bounds and serve according to the Lord's direction. What we need to consider, or be aware of, is that inspiration we receive could be from angels. There will be times, as will be shown in following chapters, where there is no question it is an angel speaking..

Donald W. Parry PhD, a professor of the Hebrew Bible in the Department of Asian and Near Eastern Languages at Brigham Young University, gave a devotional speech in which he made this statement: "It is my understanding—based on more than twenty years of research—that operations and ministrations of angels are largely unknown to mortals. Angels can move about the earth conducting the Lord's divine work, and they serve, minister, and mingle among mortals, unusually without our awareness. Most of us in mortality will never see an angel. As Parley P. Pratt instructed, angels can 'be present without being visible to mortals.'"[23]

In discussing who the ministering angels are and where our inspiration is coming from, let us also consider how they communicate with us.

Whether we are being influenced by the Holy Ghost or angels, the communication from them is not limited to mere words. In fact, there may be few words heard, but great truths and information conveyed.

President Packer tells us how powerful and informative these communications with angels can be: "Should an angel converse with you, neither you nor he would be confined to corporeal sight or sound in order to communicate. For there is that spiritual process described by the Prophet Joseph by which pure intelligence can flow into our minds and by which we can know what we need to know without either the effort of study or the passage of time, because that is revelation."[24]

There is one other consideration when trying to decide if the inspiration you are receiving is from an angel, the Holy Ghost, or the Lord Himself. In the scriptures, Jesus Christ often spoke in behalf of

Heavenly Father. This is called divine investiture. Jesus Christ is the Father by divine investiture. Elder Neal A. Maxwell, of the Quorum of the Twelve Apostles, confirmed this principle of divine investiture with the example of Jesus Christ representing the Father: "Through a process of divine investiture, most of the words of our Heavenly Father have come to us through His only Begotten Son, Jesus Christ. Because there are only a few special circumstances in which we have the Father's words."[25]

You might ask the question, did Heavenly Father answer my prayers or did Jesus Christ? It would not matter because the answer would be the same. This same idea holds true for inspiration from the Holy Ghost or from an angel assigned to deliver the message. An angel speaks by the power of the Holy Ghost. An angel may even be sent to speak in behalf of the Lord. We may feel as though the Lord has given us an impression or a thought when in all actuality a ministering angel was authorized to deliver that message. The pronouncement still comes from the Lord because he sent His messenger to deliver the message, but the medium used was a ministering angel.

The Bible Dictionary says, "There are many references to the work of angels in the Old Testament. In some passages the *'angel of the Lord' speaks as the voice of God himself*" (Bible Dictionary, "Angels"; emphasis added).

The Bible Dictionary references the example of the angel appearing to Abraham after he had obeyed the Lord's request to sacrifice Isaac and speaking as if he, the angel, was the Lord.

> "And the angel of the Lord called unto him out of heaven, and said, Abraham, Abraham: and he said, Here am I.
>
> And he said, Lay not thine hand upon the lad, neither do thou anything unto him: for now I know that thou fearest God, seeing thou hast not withheld thy son, thine only son from me" (Genesis 22:11–12).

The scriptures give us another example of this very scenario. An angel was sent to speak for Jesus Christ, or at least John the Revelator responded as if he were Jesus Christ, when in reality it was an actual angel acting in behalf of the Lord. As the messenger delivers the information, John falls to the earth and begins to worship the angel. The angel responded to this by saying, "See thou do it not: I am thy fellow-servant, and of thy brethren that have a testimony of Jesus: worship God: for the testimony of Jesus is the spirit of prophecy" (Revelation 19:10).[26]

Angels may speak for the Lord or appear to be Him because they are of one heart and mind with the Father's purposes.

I don't know if the inspiration I received one day while fulfilling my Relief Society responsibilities was from the Holy Ghost or from an angel, but my visit was heaven-sent to a sister I will call Alice. I went to visit a sister that lived in an upstairs apartment of the home where Alice lived. After a nice visit with the sister upstairs, I left. I then had the impression to knock on Alice's door, the sister that owned the home. I immediately began to rationalize why I should not go knock on her door. (Sometimes we are not very cooperative angels.) I didn't know if she was there, and if she was there, she was probably busy. I had so many things to get done that day. I got in the car and actually started backing out of her driveway. Once again I felt like I needed to go see her. I pulled back in and went to the door where she welcomed me in. After visiting for a time she said, "Why did you come to my door?" I said, "I don't know, I felt like I should." She said, "When I saw you arrive, I hoped that you had come to see me but you went upstairs and then you started to drive away. I needed to see you today. Thank you for coming back." Alice was sweet enough to share with me that she had needed me that day. I was grateful I had gone back.

Would it not be a great comfort and blessing to each of us to know that angels are there? Would that not testify to us of our Heavenly Father's love and concern for us? Elder Bruce C. Hafen, a member of the First Quorum of the Seventy, said, "Other personal manifestations have been so quiet that those who received them were unaware of the angelic presence. The ministry of these unseen angels is among the most sublime forms of interaction between heaven and earth, powerfully expressing God's concern for us and bestowing tangible assurance and spiritual sustenance upon those in great need. . . . The veil between heaven and earth usually hides the angels from our sight."[27]

We serve each other as angels, but who might the angels be that come from the other side of the veil to minister to us? Who would want to see us succeed in this life? Who are those angels that would feel pain and sorrow for us? Those angels who come to us surely love us and have our best interest at heart. The Doctrine and Covenants teaches us that "there are no angels who minister to this earth but those who do belong or have belonged to it" (D&C 130:5). So the angels that would care about us have lived on this earth.

Joseph Smith taught, "When men are prepared, they are better off to go hence [into the spirit world]. Brother Adams has gone to open up a more effectual door for the dead. Enveloped in flaming fire, they are not far from us, and know and understand our thoughts, feelings, and motions, and are often pained therewith."[28]

So angels know of our struggles and feel our pain. The angels that come to us may be our deceased fathers and mothers, our brothers and sisters, or our children and friends. President Joseph F. Smith said, "In like manner our fathers and mothers, brothers, sisters and friends who have passed away from this earth, having been faithful, and worthy to enjoy these rights and privileges, may have a mission given them to visit their relatives and friends upon the earth again, bringing from the divine Presence messages of love, of warning, or reproof and instruction, to those whom they had learned to love in the flesh."[29]

Whoever those angels are, they love us and are concerned about the challenges we face. From President Smith's statement we learn that they may come to correct us and warn us.

In the *Deseret News*, Daniel Peterson shared a story of angels that came to prepare their friends, in a similar situation, for the step they were about to take into the spirit world. This story reveals the love and concern of heavenly angels.

Ken and Debbie McCarty lived in our ward so this story has special meaning to me. Sarah, their daughter, died in 1997 after fighting a battle with cystic fibrosis. She was 13 years old.

When Sarah was nine, her parents took her on a cruise in Russia.

It was while she was on this cruise that she had a remarkable experience. Sarah had developed a strong friendship with Kerie, a 32-year-old woman who had been diagnosed with terminal melanoma, a skin cancer that is fatal. Despite the age difference their common fight for life had built a special connection between the two friends.

Two weeks into the cruise, Sarah entered her parent's room in tears. Sarah was so shaken that she could not stop crying. Finally she informed her parents that her dear friend, Kerie, had died.

How did Sarah know this? They had no contact with friends back home. Sarah explained that while she was having her evening prayers Kerie had appeared to her. Kerie relayed her message to Sarah not through words in her ears but words felt in her heart. Kerie wanted Sarah to not fear dying because it was beautiful. She also didn't want Sarah to worry about her because she was happy.

Kerie's death was confirmed by her father, Wes Waters, when they returned from the cruise. Sarah had seen her friend 30 minutes after she had died.

Cystic fibrosis continued to take its toll on Sarah's health weakening her body. When Sarah took her final breath at 6:17 a.m. on a beautiful April morning, her parents decided to wait until 8:30 a.m. to notify their loved ones that Sarah had passed away. At 8:00 a.m. the phone rang. It was Don Wood, a 42-year-old man that also suffered with cystic fibrosis. He was one of the longest survivors of the disease in the United States. Ken and Debbie had not been in contact with Don for several years yet he called on the morning Sarah died.

He knew Sarah had passed away around 6:30 that morning. Ken was shocked that Don knew about Sarah's passing because they had not notified anyone about her dying. Don said,

> "I was lying in my bed struggling to breathe. . . . I've been on oxygen for some time now, and I wasn't sure if I would last through the night. At around 6:30 I felt a presence in my room, and, when I looked up, I saw Sarah standing in the air at the foot of my bed. I thought she was coming to take me to the other side, but I was surprised to see her because I didn't know she had passed away. She was all aglow, and it looked as if light was emanating from her, not just from around her; her entire being was glowing. Her hair was long

> and curled and she looked beautiful and mature. She didn't talk out loud, but she communicated with me in a clear voice in my mind. She simply said, 'I came to tell you, Don, don't be afraid to die. It's not scary. I came to tell you that heaven is beautiful."
>
> "Sarah looked happy and beautiful," Don said, "and healthier than he had ever seen her."
>
> Eight months after Sarah died, Don Wood, too, passed away.
>
> "For some people," Ken McCarty summarizes, "life after death is a hope, something to have faith in. For me, because of our little Sarah, it's a fact. And, most important of all, it's beautiful."[30]

Who are the angels? They are our family, friends, and neighbors who serve each other. They are spirits that are unembodied, disembodied, or persons that are re-embodied (resurrected) or translated. Paul warned us, "Be not forgetful to entertain strangers: for thereby some have entertained angels unawares" (Hebrews 13: 2).

Keep in mind you may serve as an angel to help give directions and guidance. That service could be inspired by the Holy Ghost or by an angel. Elder Jeffrey R. Holland summed it up this way, "In the gospel of Jesus Christ we have help *from both sides of the veil.*"[31]

The purpose of this book is to make us aware that angels are our associates. In the pages that follow we will learn the role that they play and how the gospel of Jesus Christ possesses the keys to the administering of angel.

Chapter 3

The Lord's Pattern

As a missionary, I heard the complaint that The Church of Jesus Christ of Latter-day Saints had a few too many angels in its history to make its beginnings believable.

When I stopped to think about it, there were a lot of manifestations of angels in the early history of the Church. At the time I wondered, would angels appearing to Joseph Smith be a valid reason for not believing that the Church was of divine origin? On the other hand, is the reason the Church is true because it was restored by angels? What other Christian organization claims that angels brought truth, authority, and knowledge to establish their church?

Joseph Smith had to be tutored from some source. He was young and open to the truth. Elder Dallin H. Oaks said, "The Prophet Joseph had no role models from whom he could learn how to be a prophet and leader of the Lord's people. He learned from heavenly messengers and from the harvest of his unique spiritual gifts."[32]

The ministering of angels has always been a vital part of God's work here on the earth. Anyone who would turn from this Church, The Church of Jesus Christ of Latter-day Saints, making a statement such as "God does not work through angels today," has not seriously read or comprehended the scriptures. God works through angels and has since the beginning of time. "Jesus Christ is the same yesterday, and to day, and for ever" (Hebrews 13:8), and angels are His primary messengers.

Elder Tad R. Callister, a member of the presidency of the Seventy, gave a talk on how the Church's organization matches the blueprint found in the New Testament. There are specific blessings that come because this Church is the same Church that Christ established while he was on the earth. One of those signs and blessing that bears testimony that this is the true Church is the ministration of angels. Elder Callister said,

> The blueprint of Christ's Church records many accounts of angels and visions. Some people look with skepticism today at a church that claims angels and visions, but in so doing forget that angels and visions were a critical part of Christ's original Church: the angel announcing the birth of Christ to Mary; the angels coming to Peter, James, and John on the Mount of Transfiguration; the angel releasing Peter and John from prison; the angel speaking to Cornelius; the angel warning Paul of the impending shipwreck; the angel coming to John the Revelator; Stephen's vision of the Father and the Son; John's vision of the last days; and many more. The question should not be 'How can The Church of Jesus Christ of Latter-day Saints be the true Church with its alleged angels and visions?' Rather, the question should be 'How can any church today claim to be Christ's true Church unless it has angels and visions—just as was the case in Christ's original Church, just as it is revealed in His blueprint?[33]

The Bible sites hundreds of examples of angels ministering to men. Take the first two chapters in Matthew and Luke as examples.

- Joseph is directed by an angel to take Mary to wife (Matthew 1:20).
- The young child, Jesus, was preserved from Herod's terrible order to destroy all males two years and younger by a message delivered by an angel to Joseph (Matthew 2:13).
- Joseph was also instructed by an angel when he could return to Israel, specifically Nazareth (Matthew 2:19).
- Zacharias saw an angel as he carried out the duties of a priest to burn incense in the temple. Zacharias and his wife Elisabeth had no children and Elisabeth and Zacharias were both "now well stricken in years" (Luke 1:7), and too old to have children. The angel told him they would have a son, and even instructed Zacharias what he was to name the child, John (Luke 1:13).

Luke names the angel that appeared to Zacharias. "I am Gabriel, that stand in the presence of God; and am sent to speak unto thee" (Luke 1:19). Gabriel was the prophet Noah.[34] He came from the world of spirits as an angel and told Mary of her special mission (Luke 1:30–31). This angel, Gabriel or Noah, was obviously still involved in a work that he loved.

Angels appeared to the shepherds to announce the birth of Jesus Christ. Can you even begin to imagine the joy you or I would experience to be chosen to hear the songs of that heavenly choir?

"The angel of the Lord came. . .. And the angel said unto them, Fear not: for, behold, I bring you good tidings of great joy. . .. And suddenly there was with the angel a multitude of the heavenly host praising God, and saying, Glory to God in the highest, and on earth peace, good will toward men" (Luke 2:9–10, 13–14).

It is apparent in the first few chapters of Matthew and Luke that angels appeared often. This was the dawning of a new dispensation. Angels helped set the stage for Christ to establish His Church on earth. Yet, no one today questions the number of appearances or why it was important that angels be the messengers. Instead we sing without even a second's hesitation Christmas songs such as "Angels We Have Heard on High" or "Hark the Herald Angels Sing." Do we put the two together? Angels were singing to men in a field.[35]

The pattern was set from the Lord's first dealings with man. When Adam and Eve were driven out of the Garden of Eden the Lord sent angels to communicate with them (Moses 5:6).

Adam was taught by angels and so were Mary, Joseph, and Zacharias, and so was Joseph Smith.

> And now, *he imparteth* his word by angels unto men, yea, not only men but women also. Now this is not all; little children do have words given unto them many times, which confound the wise and the learned. (Alma 32:23; emphasis added)

I was raised in the Church and I easily accepted its divine origin. However, I was shocked to find hundreds of references to angels in the standard works. I had never stopped and studied the many times the Bible and our companion scriptures talked about angels.

I thought it was something unique to the Restoration of the gospel. Instead I was amazed at the many times angels have played significant roles throughout all of man's history. The role of angels in the beginning of the restored Church was not unique at all.

The Lord's pattern is clear. If the knowledge and authority is not already on the earth, He sends messengers. Elder L. Tom Perry explained the necessity of all those heavenly messengers being sent to a very young Joseph Smith. "In order to organize the work to begin this dispensation, the Lord needed a pure spirit, unlearned in the things of the world, one who could be taught by the ministration of angels, for there was no earthly teacher equipped to do this training."[36]

What a great witness that this is God's Church, once again restored by His hand through the aid of heavenly messengers. Joseph didn't read the Bible and figure out a scheme for a new church. The Lord sent heavenly messengers to teach him as He has always done in the past. In the Doctrine and Covenants, the Lord stated that He used angels to teach the prophets from "Adam to Abraham, from Abraham to Moses, from Moses to Jesus and his apostles, and from Jesus and his apostles to Joseph Smith, whom I did call upon by mine angels, my ministering servants, and by mine own voice out of the heavens, to bring forth my work" (D&C 136:37).

Joseph Smith's death served as a witness that this Church is true and that angels did indeed minister to him. Joseph's final testimony confirms the truth of the reality of the ministration of angels: "Joseph bore a powerful testimony to the guards of the divine authenticity of the Book of Mormon, the restoration of the Gospel, the administration of angels, and that the kingdom of God was again established upon the earth, for the sake of which he was then incarcerated in that prison, and not because he had violated any law of God or man."[37]

One of the principles we can learn from all these scriptural examples is that we can have the same experiences. David M. McConkie, first counselor in the Sunday School general presidency said, "The long-awaited restitution of all things had begun, and the principle of revelation was everlastingly established in our dispensation. Joseph's message, and our message to the world, can be summarized in two words: 'God speaks.' He spoke anciently, He spoke to Joseph, and He will speak to you."[38]

The communication from the Lord comes in many different ways, but we need to be aware that one of those ways is through angels. Joseph Smith's experience with angels does not need to be unique to him. If the need arises, angels can be sent to us.

I liked the way Joseph Fielding McConkie, an emeritus professor of Ancient Scripture at Brigham Young University, stated this same principle:

> The prophetic efforts of Joseph Smith did not center in sharing his spiritual experiences but rather in the effort to qualify us to have our own spiritual experiences. The emphasis of his ministry was not on what he had seen but on what we could see. . . . We have a dozen revelations in the Doctrine and Covenants that invited us to see God. Joseph invited us to check him by having our own Sacred Grove experience. The validity of an experiment is if it can be repeated. A good seed not only bears good fruits but it always bears the same fruits—regardless of who plants it. The true test of a prophet and seer does not rest in his conveying his revelations, but in his qualifying you to receive your own.[39]

The existence of angels may seem very foreign to some. Without understanding that the Lord has always used angels, some might respond as the following author did on the news. Elder Jeffrey R. Holland shared a statement that reflects the attitude of some in the world today. Hopefully, we have not individually dismissed the role of angels in our lives.

> On a recent news show an author who had just written a book about belief in God was being questioned about whether he personally believed in God.
>
> The author answered with something like this: 'If I knew whether or not I believed in God, I wouldn't have had to write this book. I have no idea whether there is a God, but I do know that religion has gotten a bad name from people who do things like worship cactus and believe in angels.' That was it. That was his whole response. He didn't know whether he believed in God or not, but believing in angels was clearly equal to worshipping cactus.[40]

If this is the prevailing attitude, it is easy to understand why some would be critical of the Church's humble beginnings. I question whether members of the Church fully understand the role of angels in God's work and in our personal lives. I know before writing this book, I did not fully appreciate the blessings angels have brought into my life.

Elder Mark E. Peterson testified that angels still play a role in revealing truth today.

> Many people no longer believe in the ministry of angels. But God does! He has used this means of communication from the days of Adam. Is there any reason why He should not continue the procedure in our day? . . .
>
> We declare that there is revelation today! There are apostles and prophets on earth now! They are inspired, and they do speak the word of God. *Marvelous and repeated angelic visitations have taken place in modern times* as God once again established His divine Church on earth, following a long period of darkness.[41]

As a religious educator, I teach how the Lord blesses and directs our lives through the gift of the Holy Ghost. Unfortunately, I rarely talk or teach of the ministration of angels and how they direct our lives. Yet, angels constitute one of the great tender mercies of the Lord and are a part of this gospel plan; they are here to bless our lives.

When I have spoken on this topic, I have asked audiences to raise their hand if they have experienced the influence of heavenly messengers in their own life. Nearly every hand is raised. Several individuals will come up after to share their remarkable experience with angelic messengers. Yet, we seldom talk of angels in our own lives or testify of their existence.

Perhaps we do not talk of angels because of the sacred nature of those experiences. President Boyd K. Packer gave us this caution: "I have come to believe also that it is not wise to continually talk of unusual spiritual experiences. They are to be guarded with care and shared only when the Spirit itself prompts you to use them to the blessing of others."[42]

Gabe's story (chapter 1) is one that we have felt prompted to share in the hope that it would be a blessing to others. We would not want this young man's communication with his mother to be seen as trite or contrived, but as an expression of God's hand in our lives. This experience shows how God is directing the labor on both sides of the veil as He works to redeem mankind. One of the blessings that have come into my life from writing this book is the knowledge of how unaware I have been of the ministration of angels. It is as if the veil covering my eyes has been slightly parted with a vision of angels working in behalf of the Lord in the past and in the present.

Gabe's message to me was that the Lord has a plan for him and his family, and I am awakened to the fact that there is also a plan for me. It is as if Gabe's message was, "I will be working to fulfill that plan in my sphere but I want my family to fulfill their part of the plan, and if needed, I will do my part to help make that happen." If others can be more aware of how many resources the Lord is using to assist us through life, and praise Him for His tender mercies in our behalf, then Gabe's story will bring honor to the giver of all good gifts.

"For behold, God knowing all things, being from everlasting to everlasting, behold, *he sent angels to minister unto the children of men*, to make manifest concerning the coming of Christ; and in *Christ there should come every good thing*" (Moroni 7:22; emphasis added).

It is truly a leap of faith when we come to realize that we need to follow the promptings we receive as the Lord tries to help us fulfill what we have been sent here to do and to learn. As mentioned earlier in Hebrews, "It is a fearful thing to fall into the hands of the living God" (Hebrew 10:31). Sometimes that leap requires us to sacrifice or experience unbearable pain along the way. But as we willingly submit to God's will, our very natures are changed. That is the message that Gabe taught me.

Maybe we do not talk more about angels because we have forgotten those sweet tender experiences. Elder Richard G. Scott warned us of the need to record sacred experiences and impressions. "Knowledge carefully recorded is knowledge available in time of need. Spiritually sensitive information should be kept in a sacred place that communicates to the Lord how you treasure it. That practice enhances the likelihood of your receiving further light."[43]

Even the scriptures remind us to keep an account of our sacred experiences lest we forget them. "Take heed to thyself, and keep thy soul diligently, lest thou forget the things which thine eyes have seen, and lest they depart from thy heart all the days of thy life" (Deuteronomy 4:9). In the moment, we may think we will never forget sacred experiences. But as time passes, those feelings and events are replaced by the demands of everyday living. We may even doubt the experiences we were given and brush them off as being "caught up in the moment."

It is also possible that we are afraid to share these sacred experiences because we are concerned that we will be misunderstood or mocked. Perhaps our understanding of angels is very different from someone else's. Some may think that angels have wings and are akin to aliens from outer space.

For example, how would you have reacted to a sweet young lady who stayed after school one day and shared the following story with you? Let's call her Joyce for this story.

Joyce seemed to be a little hesitant to share her feelings with me. I think she was worried that I would consider her strange or unusual. She said, "Sister Anthony, I have a special gift. I can see spirits." She waited to see if I would criticize her or discount her gift. I said, "That is really a special blessing you have been given." She seemed to relax and was then ready to share with me. She went on to explain that this gift of seeing spirits was made manifest in her life even as a very young child and she shared several examples. She said she has one particular angel, she called him a spirit, that is never far from her and she sees him often. She then said, "Last year, I started doing some things I should not have been doing. I told my mom this year that I didn't want to sign up for seminary. My mom signed me up anyway. I was mad at her. I came to your class hesitantly but I want you to know that I love being here." She then glanced down and preceded, "Your room is full of spirits. I feel them every time I come to seminary. I love to be here." This brought tears to my eyes.

Then my student, Joyce, went on to tell me how grateful she was that she had come back to seminary. She had stayed to thank me, but as most seminary teachers know, it is not you they should be thanking. It is the Holy Ghost that should be thanked for bearing witness to them. She had allowed the Spirit once again into her heart. She told me of a dream she had during the time she was going against those things she knew to be right. In the dream, Joyce saw the Savior's face. He was asking her, "Why are you doing these things?" She said, "His eyes were filled with sorrow." She then explained that as she was distancing herself from the gospel that the angel that followed her kept looking down. She said, "He was really starting to bug me." She was grateful that she was on her way back into full activity because she was once again at harmony with those spirits around her.

Her experiences reminded me of one of the spiritual gifts recounted in the book of Moroni. "And again, to another, the beholding of angels and ministering spirits" (Moroni 10:14). She seemed to have been given that special gift of beholding angels and ministering spirits. I was talking to her new teacher one day and I said, "Joyce is a very special young lady. She has been given the gift of being able to see spirits." Her new teacher replied, "I know, she shared an experience with me. You know what, I believe her." I said, "I do too."

Whatever reason is given, we seldom speak of the ministering of angels. When I have felt the influence of heavenly beings, I have felt that this experience may have been unique to me. I was unaware that angels have always played a vital role in the lives of those who love the Lord. I hope the upcoming chapters in this book will open our eyes to the fact that angels are ministering to the world today as they always have. The ministration of angels shows the Lord's incredible desire and ability to guide and direct each one of us in our own personal way.

Chapter 4

The Gift of the Holy Ghost

Volumes have been written explaining the role of the Holy Ghost in our lives. I address it here to make sure that the role of the Holy Ghost is not overlooked and devalued as the greatest type of revelation and guidance in our lives. This book is about angels, but the Holy Ghost is the great revelator. As wonderful as it is to have the ministering of angels, as members of the Church of Jesus Christ of Latter-day Saints, we know that the blessing of having the constant companionship of the Holy Ghost is the greatest gift we can be given in this life.

Remember, while the theme of this book is angels, it is by the Holy Ghost that angels speak. The Holy Ghost serves as a constant companion if we live worthy.

As the third member of the Godhead, the Holy Ghost's mission is to witness to us that Jesus is our Savior. The Holy Ghost will teach us "the truth of all things" (Moroni 10:5). President Joseph Fielding Smith explained that the Holy Ghost is so convincing that He leaves us with no doubt: "When a man has the manifestation from the Holy Ghost, it leaves an indelible impression on his soul, one that is not easily erased. It is Spirit speaking to spirit, and it comes with convincing force. A manifestation of an angel, or even the Son of God himself, would impress the eye and mind, and eventually become dimmed, but the impressions of the Holy Ghost sink deeper into the soul and are more difficult to erase."[44]

On another occasion President Smith said, "Through the Holy Ghost the truth is woven into the very fiber and sinews of the body so that it cannot be forgotten."[45]

The gift of the Holy Ghost is a sacred gift given to worthy members of the Church. When we were confirmed members of the Church, we were told to "receive the Holy Ghost." "The gift of the Holy Ghost is the right to have, whenever one is worthy, the companionship of the Holy Ghost. For those who receive this gift, the Holy Ghost acts as a cleansing agent to purify them and sanctify them from all sin" (Bible Dictionary, "Holy Ghost").

President Wilford Woodruff testifies that the Holy Ghost is the greatest gift given to man:

> Now, if you have the Holy Ghost with you—and every one ought to have—I can say unto you that there is no greater gift, there is no greater blessing, there is no greater testimony given to any man on earth. You may have the administration of angels; you may see many miracles; you may see many wonders in the earth; but I claim that the gift of the Holy Ghost is the greatest gift that can be bestowed upon man. It is by this power that we have performed that which we have. It is this that sustains us through all the persecutions, trials and tribulations that come upon us.[46]

Brigham Young had an angel, Joseph Smith, appear to him to teach him how important it is for us to have the constant companionship of the Holy Ghost. President Brigham Young recorded the following on February 23, 1847, at Winter Quarters: "While sick and asleep about noonday of the 17th, I dreamed that I went to see Joseph. He looked perfectly natural, sitting with his feet on the lower round of his chair. . . . Joseph stepped toward me, and looking very earnestly, yet pleasantly said, 'Tell the people to be humble and faithful, and be sure to keep the spirit of the Lord and it will lead them right.'"[47]

Having and keeping the Holy Ghost in our lives should be our goal. The Holy Ghost changes us. One of my favorite quotes concerning the Holy Ghost comes from Parley P. Pratt. His quote demonstrates our dire need to have the Holy Ghost as a constant companion.

> The gift of the Holy Ghost . . . quickens all the intellectual faculties, increases, enlarges, expands and purifies all the natural passions and affections; and adapts them, by the gift of wisdom, to their lawful use. It inspires, develops, cultivates and matures all the fine-toned sympathies, joys, tastes, kindred feelings, and affections of our nature. It inspires virtue, kindness, goodness, tenderness, gentleness, and charity. It develops beauty of person, form and features. It tends to health, vigor, animation, and social feeling. It invigorates all the faculties of the physical and intellectual man. It strengthens, and gives tone to the nerves. In short, it is, as it were, marrow to the bone, joy to the heart, light to the eyes, music to the ears, and life to the whole being.[48]

Having the companionship of the Holy Ghost makes one happy. One of my favorite experiences as a seminary teacher is having students I taught tell me about their mission call and occasionally having them come back after their mission and report to me. I always invite them to the front of the class to bear their testimony. They always bring such a powerful spirit into the room. There have been some dramatic changes in some of my students. I remember one young man telling me, "I am so happy." I asked him if he wasn't happy in high school. He said, "There were a few things I needed to take care of. I thought I was happy in high school, but I didn't even know what happiness was!"

You feel different, you act different, and you look different when you have the Spirit. There are so many people worried today about their looks. The best beauty secret I have observed is the glow that comes from having the Spirit. It is really hard to find a missionary that isn't handsome or a sister missionary that is not beautiful. The Spirit does exactly what Elder Pratt says: "It develops beauty of person, form and features."[49]

You can tell when you have the Holy Ghost in your life by the fruits of your actions. President Gordon B. Hinckley outlined how we would know if the Spirit is in our lives. "You recognize the promptings of the Spirit by the fruits of the Spirit—that which enlighteneth, that which buildeth up, that which is positive and affirmative and uplifting and leads us to better thoughts and better words and better deeds is of the Spirit of God. That which tears us down, which leads us into forbidden paths—that is of the adversary. I think it is just that plain, just that simple."[50]

Having the companionship of the Holy Ghost opens the doors to many of God's greatest tender mercies—including the ministration of angels. We are such a blessed people.

Chapter 5

Angels Help Achieve God's Plan

Elder Jeffrey R. Holland stated, "I am convinced that one of the profound themes of the Book of Mormon is the role and prevalence and central participation of angels in the gospel story."[51] How prevalent is the participation of angels? I had never stopped to look at the Book of Mormon through that lens of inquiry until I started my study of angels. The Book of Mormon outlines specific responsibilities that angels fulfill. If one of the Book of Mormon themes is to teach us the role of angels, then we should find what those responsibilities are.

Messengers are sent to teach us about the plan of redemption and to prepare us to enter into God's glory.

> [God] saw that it was expedient that man should know concerning the things whereof he had appointed unto them;
>
> Therefore *he sent angels to converse with them*, who caused men to behold of his glory.
>
> And they began from that time forth to call on his name; therefore God conversed with men, and made known unto them the plan of redemption, which had been prepared from the foundation of the world; and this he made known unto them according to their faith and repentance and their holy works. (Alma 12:28–30; emphasis added)

After Adam and Eve partook of the fruit of the tree of good and evil, the Lord in His great mercy gave them a probationary time to learn, repent, and choose good. Heavenly messengers were sent to Adam and Eve so that they could be taught about the authority of God, the plan of redemption, and His great love.

In those last few words in Alma 12:30, we learn that knowledge from God can only come to those that have faith, repent, and live righteously. We are taught only as much as we are willing to accept. The angel sent to teach us about God's glory might be our Sunday School teacher, our young women or young men advisor, our seminary or institute teacher, or even a good friend. If the message is being given but we are mentally or spiritually refusing to listen to the "angel's" message, their words will be meaningless.

Earlier in that same chapter, Alma taught, "And therefore, he that will harden his heart, the same receiveth the lesser portion of the word; and he that will not harden his heart, to him is given the greater portion of the word, until it is given unto him to know the mysteries of God until he know them in full" (Alma 12:10).

We need to have a desire to learn. If angels are sent to help us behold God's glory according to our faith and holy works, what happens if we are so distracted by the world around us that we aren't paying attention? We learn by faith and are given greater knowledge as we act on our faith.

If there is one lesson I have learned as a teacher, it is unless a student puts forth an effort to learn, it does not seem to happen. The sad reality is that whatever they have chosen to do instead of learning can actually interfere with someone else trying to learn. I have a strong testimony of what Elder David A. Bednar said: "Learning by faith cannot be transferred from an instructor to a student through a lecture, a demonstration, or an experiential exercise; rather, a student must exercise faith and act in order to obtain the knowledge for himself or herself."[52] The same would hold true for a message from an angel.

We must exercise faith and act to obtain knowledge from any source. There are various ways that we signal to the Spirit that we really don't want to learn. We indicate to the Holy Ghost that we are not going to learn right now when we refuse to sing the hymn, when we bring the cares of the world with us to class, sleep through the class, do other homework, or spend our time on cell phones playing games, looking at Facebook, and texting. These distractions block our ability to feel and hear. Instead of basking in the warmth of the Spirit as it falls over us, some turn off the flow of their blessings and sit out in the cold and wonder why they don't feel the whispering and promptings of spiritual communication. The warmth is there, but they choose not to feel it. Laman and Lemuel refused to hear or feel. "Ye have seen an angel, and he spake unto you; yea, ye have heard his voice from time to time; and he hath spoken unto you in a still small voice, but ye were past feeling, that *ye could not feel his words.*" (1 Nephi 17:45; emphasis added).

It is obvious that if we are not prepared to learn about God's glory, it will not matter who is serving as that angelic messenger; we will not be ready to learn or to feel unless we prepare and invest ourselves.

Angels call men to repent.

Moroni, quoting the teachings of his father, Mormon, asked if miracles have ceased. After stating they have not, he adds,

> Neither have angels ceased to minister unto the children of men.
>
> For behold, they are subject unto him, to minister according to the word of his command. . . . And the *office of their ministry is to call men unto repentance*, and to fulfil and to do the work of the covenants of the Father, which he hath made unto the children of men, to prepare the way among the children of men, by declaring the word of Christ unto the chosen vessels of the Lord, that they may bear testimony of him. (Moroni 7:29–31; emphasis added)

"Repentance means overcoming sin by changing your heart, attitudes, and actions."[53] Angels are there to help us make that change. Elder Jeffrey R. Holland counseled us to request the help of angels as we try to overcome our addictions. Keep in mind that *all* sin is addictive. "Acknowledge that people bound by the chains of true addictions often need more help than self-help, and that may include you. Seek that help and welcome it. Talk to your bishop. Follow his counsel. Ask for a priesthood blessing. Use the Church's Family

Services offerings or seek other suitable professional help. Pray without ceasing. *Ask for angels to help you*."[54]

President Boyd K. Packer also confirmed that angels can be called upon to help us repent. "The twin principles of repentance and forgiveness exceed in strength the awesome power of the tempter. If you are bound by a habit or an addiction that is unworthy, you must stop conduct that is harmful. *Angels will coach you*, and priesthood leaders will guide you through those difficult times."[55]

Nephi gave up the judgment seat so he, with his brother Lehi, could preach the word of God. Helaman, their father, had taught them the words of Amulek: "therefore he hath sent his angels to declare the tidings of the conditions of repentance" (Helaman 5:11).

We can ask our Heavenly Father for the extra support we need to overcome those sins that have become ingrained in our character. With angels to help us, we need never say, "This is just the way I am!" What a great asset it can be to have angels coaching and cheering us on.

It could also be a frightening experience to have an angel intervene directly in calling us to repent, as in the account of Alma the Younger and the sons of Mosiah. An angel appeared to them and commanded them to repent.

"And now Alma and those that were with him fell again to the earth, for great was their astonishment; for with their own eyes they had beheld an angel of the Lord; and his voice was as thunder, which shook the earth; and they knew that there was nothing save the power of God that could shake the earth and cause it to tremble as though it would part asunder." (Mosiah 27:18).

An angel shaking the earth would certainly be more profound than the still small voice, or so you might think. Later in the book of Alma, however, we discover that Alma did not give the angel credit for his conversion. Instead, he taught that he gained his testimony through fasting and praying many days (see Alma 5:45–47).

Gabe's birth and short sojourn on earth played a significant part in Dan (name has been changed) overcoming an addiction he had been fighting for years. He went through a change of heart that was brought on by this littlest of angels. The total impact of Gabe's life might never be known but the impact he had on Dan's life is known. Perhaps this was part of Gabe's short mission in mortality. When Dan came to the hospital Gabe had already died. The Spirit started a change in that man's heart that was facilitated by Gabe. It was truly a miracle. Here is his account.

Sweet Baby Gabe

> The start of my story for sweet baby Gabe begins earlier for me. I grew up in what most people would call a rough upbringing. I was always told what's right from wrong, but that is the funny thing about talking, you're just telling someone those things instead of showing them (walking the walk). I will sum up the last 10 years in a few short paragraphs.
>
> I grew up LDS but was never active. I always knew that I should be more into Church but with the poor influence from my parents and a few friends, I started rebelling more and more. I started off with late night partying, smoking, drinking, and getting high. Then with the passing of time my taste for partying and getting high grew into a monster. The more I did the more I wanted to do. The next step was new friends and new drugs and more and more partying. It was funny that the people who I called my friends were anything but my friends. I can't put any of the blame on them. I had the power of choice and I chose to hang out with the people I did and do the things I did.
>
> About eight or nine years ago, I started taking painkillers because I raced motocross and got injured a lot. I was always getting more and more pills. That turned out to be the biggest mistake of my life. From there I was introduced to a painkiller that is used for major back injuries and cancer patients. That painkiller was OxyContin. That pill changed my life and many of my friends and others. From there I struggled with a major opiate addiction. I started snorting it, which lead to smoking it, and then I had someone show me how to use it in other ways. My friend proceeded to tell me it's the best feeling ever! He was right . . . so I thought. My addiction grew and my habits got very expensive. Put a small family on top of that, and it was hard. The same friend introduced me to the king of all drugs, heroin. Several years of hard drugs and I never once overdosed, went to jail, or stole from anyone. You could say I was an addict with a conscience (if that makes sense). I always kept my job and paid my bills but in the back of my mind I knew that I needed to straighten

out my life and get back into the Church. My *amazing* wife held in there and *never* gave up on me, not to mention a few other key people.

I started trying to quit on my own. I never wanted to go to a rehab because I saw all of my friends go in and out of rehab and start right back up. Another reason I believe I didn't go to rehab was that God had a plan for me. The story of sweet baby Gabe comes in as I was trying to end my drug use. When I heard that Lisa was pregnant with a boy, I was happy for them. A few months later they went in for an ultrasound and it showed that something was wrong with the baby who I now call sweet baby Gabe. He had a very rare disorder called anencephaly, which meant he was going to be born without a cranial cap or a brain; all he had there was a brain stem. They were given the option by the doctor to abort Gabe, but with the counsel of their bishop and a *huge* amount of courage, they decided to go full term with Gabe. At the time I thought they were crazy. The more I learned about him and the amazing story Lisa told about Gabe, I was so happy they did what they did. It was amazing to me that Adam and Lisa were willing to follow the Spirit and put their own needs and feelings aside and help sweet baby Gabe fulfill his mission on earth.

We went to the hospital after Adam gave Gabe a name and a blessing and a few short minutes after Gabe passed away. I was very scared and I didn't know what to expect or think about this whole thing, or the concept of holding a baby that had passed away; I was scared. I didn't want to go. If that's how I felt, I wondered how Adam, Lisa, and sweet baby Gabe felt. We walked in the room and I immediately felt something. I walked into that hospital room and immediately I felt the very hand of Christ holding the whole room. Even me, who had been in the darkest of places in my past, felt the Spirit there. Still to this day, that strong feeling has never hit me as hard as it did then. When it was my turn to hold sweet Gabe, the best way I can describe it was like he was holding me. I felt so at peace and I felt like it was just he and I in the room. It's hard for me to talk about, but I believe that sweet, sweet Gabe's mission and his choice to come to earth was to save me! I struggled with it for a minute, but the feeling of the Spirit overcame me and I knew that Gabe had come to change my life and he *did*!

After that night I went home, and I felt the Spirit so imprinted on me that I stayed awake all night. With the help of my *amazing* wife, some of my family, and also a great neighbor, I started going

> to Church to change my life. A little while later I tried to figure out what I was trying to accomplish or cover up or hide. I think at first my drugs were fun. Then over time I used more and more. Life became hard to live, at least what most people call a normal life: going to work, church, family, etc. How could you be happy and free of drugs? It was like I was chasing happiness but I couldn't catch it. The feeling is like being on top of the world all the time no matter what is going on in your life. If I was in trouble or fights, had arguments, bills to pay, or if I was short money, had family problems, none of it mattered because you always had something to mask the pain, mask the regret and the feeling of being lost and alone. So we went to Church. We went to the temple and received our endowments and were sealed as a family of five! That day turned out to be one of the greatest moments of my life. The feeling that I received by choosing the right and going through the temple was more than any drug could ever do for me.
>
> I now have a feeling of peace. I don't have to chase the happiness that was so temporary with drugs. There is no greater feeling than being moved by the Spirit. I know it's different for everyone, but for me, I had never felt anything up until this point. I was now on cloud 9! And I haven't come down yet. I have been clean since October 13, 2008, and I've never looked back since. It's been amazing to think I have overcome one of the hardest temptations to overcome, with the help of sweet baby Gabe and a few other key people. Now that I'm free from my drug addiction, I wake up every morning thanking my Heavenly Father for all that he has done for me and continues to do. Now I own a very successful website and do marketing and sales for a multimillion dollar company in the health care industry. With my website business and my day job, I get to help people change their lives by planting seeds of hope and giving them dreams.
>
> To this day I love sharing my story and helping others, especially others that have the same problems I had. There are so many people like me out there!

Just fourteen months after Gabe passed, Dan knelt across the altar in the temple and was sealed with his wife for all eternity. The Spirit testified to all those witnessing this special event of the importance of eternal families. The spirit that filled the room when their three young children were brought in and sealed to their parents for eternity cannot be described. Five years later, Dan and his wife had their fourth child, Josiah, born under the covenant. This sweet little

Josiah was born at 34 weeks and lived just long enough for Dan to be able bless this child before he passed back to the other side of the veil. Josiah was blessed to be able to be born into an eternal family and have the promise of a forever family. The choices you make each day can have an everlasting impact. Maybe Gabe's birth not only helped spark the flame of change in Dan's life but also prepared them for their own challenge.

"The office of their [angels'] ministry is to call men unto repentance" (Moroni 7:31). Angels don't just call us to repent, they rejoice with us as we conquer our weaknesses through Christ. "Likewise, I say unto you, there is joy in the presence of the angels of God over one sinner that repenteth" (Luke 15:10).

As our very natures are changed through repentance and we are filled with the Spirit and bear testimony of the Savior's power to cleanse us, our testimony is recorded for those on the other side of the veil to look upon. "Nevertheless, ye are blessed, for the testimony which ye have borne is recorded in heaven for the angels to look upon; and they rejoice over you, and your sins are forgiven you" (D&C 62:3). If you want angels to rejoice in heaven, repent and bear your testimony.

Angels serve the Lord in fulfilling His plan.

Moroni 7:31 points out another role angels play besides helping us to repent; it is "to *fulfil and to do the work of the covenants of the Father*, which he hath made unto the children of men" (emphasis added). Have you ever wondered if God's promises will be fulfilled? Angels have the responsibility to aid the Lord in fulfilling His promises.

I made covenants in the temple of God at the time I was sealed to my eternal companion. Part of that covenant promised me that if I lived faithful that I would have my family sealed to me for all eternity. I lean heavily on those promises as I watch my family and myself struggle against odds that seem impossible to surmount. Can the Lord really make that happen in my life? What a comfort that phrase gives that I am not fighting this battle by myself. Angels are involved in that fight. I know that without the help of angels on the other side, the temple covenant will not be realized for my family and me.

President Wilford Woodruff, the fourth prophet of the Church, gave a talk illustrating how involved angels are in helping "to fulfill and to *do the work of the covenants of the Father*, which he hath made unto the children of men" (Moroni 7:31). Surely there are many angels continually involved in our Heavenly Father's great cause. This account was given in October 1880's general conference.

> I believe the eyes of the heavenly hosts are over this people; I believe they are watching the elders of Israel, the prophets and apostles and men who are called to bear off this kingdom. I believe they watch over us all with great interest.
>
> I will here make a remark concerning my own feelings. After the death of Joseph Smith I saw and conversed with him many times in my dreams in the night season. On one occasion he and his brother Hyrum met me when on the sea going on a mission to England. I had Dan Jones with me. He received his mission from Joseph Smith before his death; and the prophet talked freely to me about the mission I was then going to perform. And he also talked to me with regard to the mission of the Twelve Apostles in the flesh, and he laid before me the work they had to perform; and he also spoke of the reward they would receive after death. And there were many other things he laid before me in his interview on that occasion. And when I awoke many of the things he had told me were taken from me, I could not comprehend them.
>
> I have had many interviews with Brother Joseph until the last 15 or 20 years of my life; I have not seen him for that length of time. But during my travels in the southern country last winter I had many interviews with President Young, and with Heber C. Kimball, and Geo. A. Smith, and Jedediah M. Grant, and many others who are dead. They attended our conference, they attended our meetings. And on one occasion, I saw Brother Brigham and Brother Heber ride in a carriage ahead of the carriage in which I rode when I was on my way to attend conference; and they were dressed in the most priestly robes. When we arrived at our destination I asked Pres. Young if he would preach to us. He said, "No, I have finished my testimony in the flesh. I shall not talk to this people any more. But (said he) I have

> come to see you; I have come to watch over you, and to see what the people are doing. Then (said he) I want you to teach the people—and I want you to follow this counsel yourself—that they must labor and so live as to obtain the Holy Spirit, for without this you cannot build up the kingdom; without the spirit of God you are in danger of walking in the dark, and in danger of failing to accomplish your calling as apostles and as elders in the church and kingdom of God. And, said he, "Brother Joseph taught me this principle." And I will here say, I have heard him refer to that while he was living.[56]

The prophets of old did not lose interest in the growth of the Church just because they died. They were involved in making sure that the Church continued to go forward to fulfill its divine mission. Brigham Young was involved in teaching President Woodruff what to tell the people. Surely angels have not stopped caring about the work.

Moroni, as an angel, helped accomplish two prophecies given in the Old Testament to fulfill God's promises. Elder Mark E. Petersen of the Quorum of the Twelve Apostles stated, "So Moroni fulfilled two biblical prophecies in coming to Joseph Smith: the fourteenth chapter of Revelation and the twenty-ninth chapter of Isaiah. He did come to earth as an angel. He did deliver to Joseph Smith the golden record which had been prepared under the direction of Almighty God. It is a new witness for the Lord Jesus Christ. It declares, as does the Bible, that Jesus of Nazareth indeed is the Son of God, our Savior and Redeemer."[57]

The angel Moroni fulfilled Isaiah's prophecies for the coming forth of the Book of Mormon and John the Revelator's prophecy of an angel flying in the "midst of heaven" (Revelation 14:6). We know that there are many others that have been placed on this earth at the right time to further the Lord's work. How can God's promises possibly fail?

Since we also act as messengers for the Lord, we need to do all in our power to fulfill promises made by the Lord. It is energizing to watch the youth of this Church step forward to serve missions to fulfill the promise given in the Doctrine and Covenants: "Behold, I will hasten my work in its time" (D&C 88:73). But that work is not only taking place on the earth, but it is also going on in the spirit world. President Thomas S. Monson said,

> We, as spirit children of our Heavenly Father, were sent to earth at this time that we might participate in hastening this great work.
>
> The Lord has never, to my knowledge, indicated that His work is confined to mortality. Rather, His work embraces eternity. I believe He is hastening His work in the spirit world. I also believe that the Lord, through His servants there, is preparing many spirits to receive the gospel. Our job is to search out our dead and then go to the temple and perform the sacred ordinances that will bring to those beyond the veil the same opportunities we have.[58]

The prophecy to hasten the Lord's work is being accomplished by heavenly angels and by temporal angels on both sides of the veil. Consider that those who receive patriarchal blessings have a responsibility to fulfill the promises given to the best of their ability, realizing that as we do our part, the Lord will make those promises come to pass. Perhaps angels will assist in helping us fulfill our individual promises.

I knew a man that had been promised in his patriarchal blessing that he would serve as a bishop in Zion. The man mocked at the promise as he chose to live outside the blessings of the gospel. This man would have been a wonderful bishop if he had followed the Lord's plan instead of selecting the right glass for his wine.

Angels are sent to direct our paths according to our "strong faith and a firm mind in every form of godliness" (Moroni 7:30). Mormon goes on to say that angels declare "the word of Christ unto the *chosen vessels* of the Lord" (Moroni 7:31; emphasis added). Wouldn't it be a tragedy for us to live unaware that we have that added help? It would be just as tragic to believe that we were somehow not worthy to ask Heavenly Father for divine help. Angels don't come to perfect people; they come to imperfect people at perfect times. We in return, having felt the Spirit, testify of the Lord's great love for us.

Some people might easily accept that President Monson, the Quorum of the Twelve Apostles, their stake president, or their bishop might receive help from angels but not ordinary people like themselves. We may be unaware of what angels can do. But even if we are unaware of angels, they are aware of us. Angels are influencing us as we perform our simple tasks. President Boyd K. Packer said, "Angels attend the rank and file of the Church. . . . Who would dare to say that angels do not now attend the rank and file of the Church who answer the calls to the mission fields, teach the classes, pay their tithes and offerings, seek for the records of their forebears, work in the temples, raise their children in faith, and have brought this work through 150 years?"[59]

In the Book of Mormon, angels are sent to prepare the people for the coming of the Savior's visit to the Americas. That visit serves as a mirror image of the Savior's Second Coming. We should not be surprised to see angels involved in preparing us for the Second Coming as they were with the people of the Book of Mormon.

> For behold, angels are declaring it unto many at this time in our land; and this is for the purpose of preparing the hearts of the children of men to receive his word at the time of his coming in his glory.
>
> And now we only wait to hear the joyful news declared unto us by the mouth of angels, of his coming; for the time cometh, we know not how soon. . . .
>
> And it shall be made known unto just and holy men, by the mouth of angels, at the time of his coming, that the words of our fathers may be fulfilled, according to that which they have spoken concerning him. (Alma 13:24–26)

The Book of Mormon helps us understand that angels can be involved in teaching us about the plan of redemption if we are teachable. When we are open to the influence of the Holy Ghost, angels, who are agents of the Holy Ghost, may be sent to teach us and prepare us to return to our Heavenly Father's presence. Angels help prepare us to enter into God's glory, and one of the ways they do that is by calling us to repent. Angels can assist us as we work to repent and change our natures. Angels are there to assist the Lord in fulfilling the covenants He has made. We likewise should do all in our power to fulfill God's promises, particularly the promises made directly to us. Carol B. Thomas, second counselor in the young women general presidency, said, "You may never see angels descending out of heaven, but I can promise you as you bear testimony and pray in your families, unseen angels will minister to you."[60]

Chapter 6

The Aaronic Priesthood Holds the Key!

Angels have influenced people of all religions and nationalities. Members of the Church are not the only ones that have an interest in or have been influenced by angels.

The subject of angels attracted viewer attention when two television shows featured a theme centered around fictional stories where angels intervened to help solve people's challenges. One was called *Highway to Heaven* and starred Michael Landon as an angel. This series ran from 1984 to 1989. The second show was called *Touched by An Angel* and stared Roma Downey as an angel. *Touched by an Angel* became one of "CBS's highest-rated series during season three and continued through season six, when it was the ninth most watched network series, with 17,190,000 viewers".[61] That show ran from 1994 to 2003. The popularity of these kinds of shows demonstrated that people have an interest in the subject of angels.

Even though people outside of the Church are influenced by angels, they do not have the priesthood of God and its attendant blessings. Elder L. Tom Perry told the priesthood brethren, "Young men of the Aaronic Priesthood, I testify to you that the Lord is bound by solemn covenant to bless your lives according to your faithfulness. If you will heed the voice of warning of the Holy Ghost and will follow His direction, you will be blessed with the ministering of angels. This blessing will add wisdom, knowledge, power, and glory to your life. This is a sure blessing promised to you by the Lord."[62]

Elder Perry emphasized a promise given to Aaronic Priesthood holders if they heed the warnings of the Holy Ghost. Aaronic Priesthood holders are promised the blessing of the ministering of angels. It is a promise given by the Lord according to faithfulness. The Aaronic Priesthood members hold the key to that blessing for the entire Church.

Oftentimes, as members of the Church, we dismiss the responsibilities of the Aaronic Priesthood and concentrate only on the responsibilities of the Melchizedek Priesthood. We read in the Doctrine and Covenants, "Why it is called the lesser priesthood is because it is an appendage, to the greater, or the Melchizedek Priesthood" (D&C 107:14). One may ask, if it is only an appendage, or an attachment, or an add-on, why is it even necessary at all? It sounds like the Aaronic Priesthood is almost an optional ingredient of a recipe.

It is easy to look past the responsibilities of the Aaronic Priesthood, deeming their service as merely preparation for the Melchizedek Priesthood. In doing so, we miss out on the important role of and the great blessings we receive because of the Aaronic Priesthood. "But there are two divisions or grand heads—one is the Melchizedek Priesthood, and the other is the Aaronic or Levitical Priesthood" (D&C 107:6). Here the Lord refers to the Aaronic Priesthood as a *grand part of the priesthood.*

The Melchizedek Priesthood is splendid. It allows us to receive the mysteries of the kingdom of God and holds the key to the knowledge of God. Because of this priesthood we can be brought back into the presence of God and see the face of God (see D&C 84:19–23).

When Moses was bringing the children of Israel to Mt. Sinai, the Lord commanded him to prepare the children of Israel to enter into His presence. Moses tried to prepare the children of Israel to behold the face of God. But the children of Israel were not prepared for that privilege. The Melchizedek Priesthood was taken from them and they were left with the Aaronic Priesthood only (see D&C 84:24–26).

The Lord gave us a glimpse into the blessings we receive from the Aaronic Priesthood. "And the lesser priesthood continued, which priesthood *holdeth the key of the ministering of angels* and the preparatory gospel" (D&C 84:26; emphasis added). Once we truly understand what the keys of the ministering of angels mean, we will begin to appreciate the great blessing that is offered to us through the Aaronic Priesthood.

John the Baptist, as an angel, appeared to Joseph Smith and Oliver Cowdery to restore the Aaronic Priesthood to the earth. When the blessing was bestowed he said,

"Upon you my fellow servants, in the name of Messiah I confer the Priesthood of Aaron, which holds the keys of the ministering of angels." (D&C 13:1).

I thought for years how great it would be to hold the Aaronic Priesthood and have access to the ministering of angels in my life. When my husband conferred the Aaronic Priesthood on our oldest son, he talked about his right to have the ministering of angels. I was envious of my son receiving the Aaronic Priesthood because I wanted that gift in my life. It is obvious from my feelings that I didn't understand how the ministering of angels functioned and how the Aaronic Priesthood opened that blessing to all members of the Church.

I am indebted to Elder Dallin H. Oaks, who, in a conference address in October 1998, taught me about the Aaronic Priesthood and the keys of the ministering of angels. Until his talk, I didn't realize that blessing was also available to me.

The blessings of the ministering of angels are not limited to those that hold the Aaronic Priesthood any more than the sealing keys bless only those that officiate as sealers in the temple. Angelic ministrations are open to all worthy members of the Church by right of those keys.

Elder Oaks explained how the blessing of the ministering of angels is given to the Church:

> What does it mean that the Aaronic Priesthood holds "the key of the ministering of angels" and of the "gospel of repentance and of baptism, and the remission of sins"? The meaning is found in the ordinance of baptism and in the sacrament. Baptism is for the remission of sins, and the sacrament is a renewal of the covenants and blessings of baptism. Both should be preceded by repentance. When we keep

> the covenants made in these ordinances, we are promised that we will always have His Spirit to be with us. The ministering of angels is one of the manifestations of that Spirit.[63]

If we are repentant when we partake of the sacrament, we renew our baptismal covenants. Then we desire to keep our lives clean and worthy so we can enjoy the influence of the Holy Ghost and therefore have the blessing of the ministering of angels.

Elder Oaks further explained,

> How does the Aaronic Priesthood hold the key to the ministering of angels? The answer is the same as for the Spirit of the Lord.
>
> In general, the blessings of spiritual companionship and communication are only available to those who are clean. As explained earlier, through the Aaronic Priesthood ordinances of baptism and the sacrament, we are cleansed of our sins and promised that if we keep our covenants we will always have His Spirit to be with us. I believe that promise not only refers to the Holy Ghost but also to the ministering of angels, for "angels speak by the power of the Holy Ghost; wherefore, they speak the words of Christ" (2 Nephi 32:3). So it is that those who hold the Aaronic Priesthood open the door for all Church members who worthily partake of the sacrament to enjoy the companionship of the Spirit of the Lord and the ministering of angels.[64]

In other words, those who receive the gift of the Holy Ghost may feel both the influence of the Spirit and have angels speak to them by the power of the Spirit. Priesthood keys are given to unlock the blessings that enrich the whole family of God. The Aaronic Priesthood keys are to bless all those that fall under the administrative blessing of those Aaronic Priesthood holders who minister to them.

Elder Neil L. Andersen explained how the covenants we receive through the priesthood give members of the Church power. He told of a sister who listened as the Primary sang "Love is Spoken Here." The second verse says, "Mine is a home where every hour is blessed by the strength of priesthood power." The sister listening made the statement to the effect that her home had never known such power.

Elder Andersen's response to her comment was

To this faithful woman and to all is that we can live every hour "blessed by the strength of priesthood power," whatever our circumstance.

We sometimes overly associate the power of the priesthood with men in the Church. The priesthood is the power and authority of God given for the salvation and blessing of all—men women, and children.

A man may open the drapes so the warm sunlight comes into the room, but the man does not own the sun or the light or the warmth it brings. . . .

All of the ordinances invite us to increase our faith in Jesus Christ and to make and keep covenants with God. As we keep these sacred covenants, we receive priesthood power and blessings.[65]

As we worthily take the sacrament, and keep these covenants we make, we are given the promise of His Spirit and the right to have the ministering of angels in our life. The power or right to these blessings comes from God, not the young man carrying the tray. The priests and deacons administer the sacrament ordinance. Our worthiness unlocks the power.

Aaronic Priesthood holders have been counseled to act as ministering angels. This quote by Elder Spencer J. Condie of the Quorum of the Seventy reminds us that the Aaronic Priesthood holds the keys to the ministering of angels but the Aaronic Priesthood holders can also serve as ministering angels.

When Joseph Smith and Oliver Cowdery received the Aaronic Priesthood under the hands of the resurrected John the Baptist, they received "the keys of the ministering of angels," and so did you when you were ordained. I pray that you wonderful young men will not only be worthy to receive ministering angels, but that you . . . will *become* a ministering angel in the lives of others as you exercise your faith in working "mighty miracles," thereby becoming a "great benefit" to your fellow beings.[66]

The gift to have the ministering of angels is given to us because of the Aaronic Priesthood. We may not recognize or accept this gift because we don't understand how angels minister to us. Elder Oaks further explained how we are blessed by ministering angels:

But the ministering of angels can also be *unseen*. Angelic messages can be delivered by a voice or merely by thoughts or feelings

> communicated to the mind. President John Taylor described "the action of the angels, or messengers of God, upon our minds, so that the heart can conceive . . . revelations from the eternal world." Nephi described three manifestations of the ministering of angels when he reminded his rebellious brothers that (1) they had "seen an angel," (2) they had "heard his voice from time to time," and (3) also that an angel had "spoken unto [them] in a still small voice" though they were "past feeling" and "could not feel his words" (1 Ne. 17:45). . . . Most angelic communications are felt or heard rather than seen.[67]

Hopefully, as we strive to be clean and worthy, we will *feel* the influence of holy angels even if we never see them. I had heavenly communication given to me at a pivotal point in my marriage. The message was delivered by thoughts and feelings communicated to my mind. Yet it was a very natural conversation. I don't know who communicated the message (the Lord, the Spirit, or an angel), but this experience demonstrates one way we can receive communication. I do know that the Lord authorized the message that was sent.

While living in Bakersfield, California, we found our lives immersed in Church service. In fact, our time was totally saturated with Church responsibilities; so much so that it would often require getting a babysitter for our two young children on Sunday because we were both in meetings and unable to be home. Once we moved from Bakersfield, we started to live like a "normal" family. Dave, my husband, was now finally able to be home in the evenings to help with the children. We had previously been so involved in our multiple callings that I had become resentful of our lack of time together, and I became guarded about losing our family time again.

You can imagine my feelings when Dave was called to visit with the stake president. They had announced that a new bishop would be called the following week. I felt so bitter I didn't even think I could sustain him or agree to a call that involved serving so many. Those awful feelings filled my soul all week. Feeling weighed down, I was doing laundry in the basement when I had the strongest impression come over me. It was as if a voice spoke to me but I didn't hear the voice with my ears but the voice was crystal clear in my thoughts. I had a conversation with the voice I heard. The experience was so intense that my heart was softened and changed forever. The thought (voice) came to me, "why wouldn't Dave make a good bishop?" I responded, "He possesses all the qualities needed to be a wonderful bishop. He is loving and concerned for others. He loves the Lord and is a good administrator." I knew the only thing he lacked was a supportive wife. My possessiveness would make it impossible for him to be successful. The voice asked me about the list of characteristics I had written in a young women's class many years before. The characteristics I desired in my future husband had all been fulfilled. Dave possessed everything which I had asked for. The most important characteristic on the list was a worthy priesthood holder. The voice told me, "You don't deserve to have him. You should have had a husband that was inactive or not a member. A husband that was willing to coddle to all your needs, one that placed you before the Lord."

The feelings that came from this experience so overwhelmed me that I felt as if I had been scolded by a parent. I was ashamed of the thoughts and feelings I had been experiencing. I found myself pleading with the Lord to take him as a bishop and let me prove I could be supportive. The voice concluded, "How can I help him to be a god unless I can mold him?"

The call came from the stake president a few days later and he was asked to be first counselor in the bishopric. There were many lonely nights spent home while he served the Lord. I never once murmured about the situation. I am sure if I had not had this experience there would have been a lot of murmuring on my part, which would have made my husband's calling very difficult for him to perform. I tried to be completely supportive. In fact, I would try and get the children to bed a little early and spend a few hours doing what I wanted to do. Those hours passed quickly and became a coveted blessing.

I felt that day like I had been disciplined by the loving hand of my Heavenly Father, or His special agent, and that He had helped me have greater vision for my life, my marriage, and my service to Him.

This conversation was so real, yet the discussion was not face-to-face nor did it come through my ears. Elder Boyd K. Packer described how such communication occurs.

> Should an angel converse with you, neither you nor he would be confined to corporeal sight or sound in order to communicate. For there is that spiritual process described by the Prophet Joseph by which pure intelligence can flow into our minds and by which we can know what we need to know without either the effort or study of the passage of time, because that is revelation. We talk about confining on little computer chips vast amounts of information; through the processes of revelation and through this language of the Spirit, tremendous amounts of inspiration and information can be given to us instantly.[68]

President Wilford Woodruff testified of the administering of angels in his life. President Woodruff said, "I have had the administration of angels in my day and time, though I never prayed for an angel. I have had, in several instances, the administration of holy angels. . .. The Lord revealed to me by vision, by revelations, and by the Holy Spirit, many things that lay before me."[69]

We likewise may not pray for angels to minister to us but it is a gift available to each of us as recipients of the Aaronic Priesthood authority and the blessings that flow to all worthy members because of that authority. If we are aware of how angels administer to us, we may be more likely to recognize and honor those covenants that enable us to experience the administering of angels.

Elder M. Russell Ballard recently admonished us to live worth of those priesthood blessings. "Our Father in Heaven is generous with His power. All men and all women have access to this power for help in their lives. All who have made sacred covenants with the Lord and who honor those covenants are eligible to receive personal revelation, to be blessed by the ministering of angels, to commune with God, to receive the fulness of the gospel, and ultimately, to become heirs alongside Jesus Christ of all our Father has."[70]

I have a new reverence for the Aaronic Priesthood. I have a greater understanding of how desperately I need the blessing of the ministering of angels and the cleansing that comes as I renew my covenants. The Melchizedek Priesthood brings me into the presence of my Father in heaven but the Aaronic Priesthood enables me to stay clean and pure so I can see Him again. The ministering of angels supports me as I face the difficulties of this life. Because of the keys of the Aaronic Priesthood, I can have not only the constant companionship of the Holy Ghost through the sacrament, but also the ministering of angels. There are truly two grand heads, the Melchizedek and the Aaronic Priesthoods, and they work harmoniously together (see D&C 107:6).

Chapter 7

Angels Teach and Instruct

Angels play several roles in our lives. From the scriptures we learn how the Lord uses angels in dealing with His children. Angels teach and instruct, prophesy, protect, warn of danger, comfort, and even sometimes destroy. In the following chapters, these roles will be explained using scripture, Church history, and modern examples. Some of the examples cross over and demonstrate more than one role.

In the examples that follow it is clear that one of angels' major roles is to teach and instruct.

As mentioned earlier in chapter 3, on patterns, we discovered that the Lord uses angels to teach his children. From the very beginning, angels taught Adam and Eve.

> And after many days an angel of the Lord appeared unto Adam, saying: Why dost thou offer sacrifices unto the Lord? And Adam said unto him: I know not, save the Lord commanded me.
>
> And then *the angel spake*, saying: This thing is a similitude of the sacrifice of the Only Begotten of the Father, which is full of grace and truth. (Moses 5:6–7; emphasis added)

In this example, Adam and Eve have an angel teach them about the Atonement of Jesus Christ. In verse 9, the Holy Ghost fell upon Adam in that same day to testify of the Father and the Son, and then the Savior speaks to them: "I am the Only Begotten of the Father, . . . as thou hast fallen thou mayest be redeemed, and all mankind, even as many as will" (Moses 5:9). Here the angel teaches, the Holy Ghost bears witness, and the Savior redeems.

There are some wonderful teaching moments between angels and mortals in the Old Testament. There is a touching exchange between an angel and Hagar. Hagar was the handmaid to Sarah. Sarah gave her handmaid to Abraham to marry when Sarah was found to be barren. This example shows us that angels are not sent only to prophets and apostles or only to men but also to all those that love the Lord and are in need, even a handmaiden.

> And the angel of the Lord found her by a fountain of water in the wilderness, by the fountain in the way to Shur.
>
> And he said, Hagar, Sarai's maid, whence camest thou? And whither wilt thou go? And she said, I flee from the face of my mistress Sarai. And the angel of the Lord said unto her, Return to thy mistress, and submit thyself under her hands.
>
> And the angel of the Lord said unto her, I will multiply thy seed exceedingly, that it shall not be numbered for multitude.
>
> And the angel of the Lord said unto her, Behold, thou art with child, and shalt bear a son, and shalt call his name Ishmael; because the Lord hath heard thy affliction. (Genesis 16:7–11)

Not only did the angel instruct Hagar to return to Sarah, but he also taught her that her child had a great destiny as well and prophesied about her posterity.

One of the complex accounts in the Old Testament is the story of Abraham being asked to sacrifice his son Isaac. This was the hardest test the Lord could have given Abraham. Abraham had almost died at the hands of his wicked father and the evil priests of Elkenah, in Egypt. Why would the Lord stir up the memory of this horrible event from Abraham's past and command him to sacrifice his own son, even the birthright son? We talk about emotional scars that can occur from an abusive childhood—surely this request must have seemed extremely revolting (See Abraham 1:11–16).

It would be interesting to know if Abraham's own rescue by an angel gave him courage to go forward with the sacrifice of his son Isaac. On the other hand, did the memory of the three virgins that died (before he was put on the altar) fill him with fear? (Abraham 1:11). He doesn't share those feelings, but a heavenly messenger was sent to save Isaac at the last minute and to teach him (us?) why the Lord had made such a request of Abraham.

> And the angel of the Lord called unto him out of heaven, and said, Abraham, Abraham: and he said, Here am I.
>
> And he said, Lay not thine hand upon the lad, neither do thou anything unto him: for now I know that thou fearest God, seeing thou hast not withheld thy son, thine only son from me. (Genesis 22:11–12)

We see the angel fulfilling two roles here. Abraham was blessed to be taught by an angel why the Lord would make such a request, and Isaac was protected from being sacrificed. This was a test of Abraham's faithfulness and obedience. Would Abraham be completely compliant to every request that the Lord made of him? Abraham proved to himself and to the Lord that the Lord could trust him. Abraham showed he would sacrifice all that he had, even his son's life if that is what the Lord asked. I am awestruck at Abraham's incredible faith. Joseph Smith's *Lectures on Faith* states, "Let us here observe, that a religion that does not require the sacrifice of all things never has power sufficient to produce the faith necessary unto life and salvation."[71]

Sister Carol B. Thomas gave us a great explanation of why the Lord would ask us to sacrifice. "Sacrifice is an amazing principle. As we willing give our time and talents and all that we possess, it becomes one of our truest forms of worship. It can develop within us a profound love for each other and our Savior, Jesus Christ. Through sacrifice our hearts can be changed; we live closer to the Spirit and have less of an appetite for things of the world."[72]

When we are called on to make sacrifices, an explanation of why the Lord would ask us to sacrifice is not always given. Abraham's story reminds us that we too need to demonstrate our faith and belief that the Lord knows what He is trying to accomplish in our individual lives as our hearts are changed and we are better able to let go of the things of this world.

Nephi was tutored by an angel when he wanted to understand his father's dream of the tree of life. "And it came to pass that I saw the heavens open; and an angel came down and stood before me; and he said unto me: Nephi, what beholdest thou?" (1 Nephi 11:14).

Then the angel taught Nephi of the significance of his father's dream. The angel walked Nephi through each part of his father's dream and taught him precept by precept. "The angel spake unto me, saying: Look! And I looked and beheld the virgin again, bearing a child in her arms" (1 Nephi 11:19–20). "The angel spake unto me again, saying: Look! . . . [Nephi] saw angels descending upon the children of men: and they did minister unto them" (1 Nephi 11:30). Nephi was again taught about the life of the Savior. "The angel spake unto me again, saying: Look! And I looked and beheld the Lamb of God that he was taken by the people; yea, the Son of the everlasting God was judged of the world." (1 Nephi 11:32) Nephi was literally given a one-on-one teaching experience with an angel.

We may wish we could be tutored by an angel, because I am sure it would be an amazing experience to be taught the scriptures by an angel. I am reminded of a quote by Hugh Nibley, who was an author, a Mormon apologist, and a professor at Brigham Young University. He said, "If you pray for an angel to visit you, you know what he'll do if he comes. He'll just quote the scriptures to you—so you know you're wasting your time waiting for what we already have."[73]

As wonderful as it would be to have an angel be your instructor, you can turn to the scriptures on a daily basis and have the Holy Ghost teach you and give you insights. We have the course material right in front of us.

The next three examples are very similar. An angel comes and teaches King Benjamin, Alma the Younger, and Samuel the Lamanite what they are to teach others. Once again the angel performs a dual role. The angel taught them what to say but also prophesied of future events.

For King Benjamin, it says, "And the things which I shall tell you are made known unto me by an angel from God" (Mosiah 3:2).

The great discourse of King Benjamin about the Savior had such an impact on the people that they had "no more disposition to do evil, but to do good continually" (Mosiah 5:2). Even today, King Benjamin's words thrill the reader as the Spirit testifies to our hearts of the plan of redemption through our Savior. All these things were made known unto King Benjamin by an angel.

The second example is Alma the Younger. Alma had a reunion with the angel that came to him and called him to repent. It was the same angel that appeared to him when he and the sons of Mosiah were rebelling against the Church. This time the angel instructed him to go back to Ammonihah and prophesy of their destruction.

> While Alma was thus weighed down with sorrow, behold an angel of the Lord appeared unto him, saying:
>
> Blessed art thou, Alma; therefore, lift up thy head and rejoice, for thou hast great cause to rejoice; for thou hast been faithful in keeping the commandments of God from the time which thou receivedst thy first message from him. Behold, I am he that delivered it unto you.
>
> And behold, I am sent to command thee that thou return to the city of Ammonihah, and preach again unto the people of the city; yea, preach unto them. Yea, say unto them, except they repent the Lord God will destroy them. (Alma 8:14–16)

The third example is Samuel the Lamanite. He and Alma were each instructed to teach of the destruction that was ahead if the people didn't repent.

> And behold, thus hath the Lord commanded me, by his angel, that I should come and tell this thing unto you; yea, he hath commanded that I should prophesy these things unto you; yea, he hath said unto me: Cry unto this people, repent and prepare the way of the Lord. (Helaman 14:9)

Adam and Eve's first teachers were angels. An angel instructed a simple handmaiden, Hagar, to return and fulfill her divine destiny. An angel taught Abraham why he was called on to sacrifice Isaac. An angel taught Nephi what his father's dream meant. An angel taught King Benjamin, Alma the Younger, and Samuel the Lamanite what they should teach the people. The examples could continue, but the point is well established in scriptures that angels are to teach.

I will now turn to Church history for examples of angels

teaching. Joseph Smith was taught by many angels. It is interesting to note that when angels appear, there can be others present but they are not aware of the visit unless the angel wills it. During the course of one night, an angel appeared three times to Joseph Smith. Yet, others in the house, and even in the same room, were unaware of the heavenly visits. The appearance of an angel seems to be very selective and visible only to those to whom the messenger wishes to appear.

On September 21, 1823, Joseph knelt in prayer asking for "a manifestation" (Joseph Smith—History 1:29) when an angel appeared to him. It was the resurrected Moroni, the last prophet to write in the Book of Mormon. Moroni taught Joseph out of the Bible (see Joseph Smith—History 1:36, 40–41).

Once again an angel used the scriptures to teach. Joseph recorded that this tutoring continued, "Accordingly, as I had been commanded, I went at the end of each year, and at each time I found the same messenger there, and received *instruction* and intelligence from him at each of our interviews, respecting what the Lord was going to do, and how and in what manner his kingdom was to be conducted in the last days" (Joseph Smith—History 1:54; emphasis added).

Moroni must have taught Joseph about the Nephite and the Lamanite people and their customs. Lucy Mack Smith, Joseph Smith's mother, wrote, "During our evening conversations, Joseph would occasionally give us some of the most amusing recitals that could be imagined. He would describe the ancient inhabitants of this continent, their dress, mode of traveling, and the animals upon which they rode; their cities, their buildings, with every particular; their mode of warfare; and also their religious worship. This he would do with as much ease, seemingly, as if he had spent his whole life among them."[74]

This same angel, Moroni, appeared and showed the plates to three other witnesses. Moroni instructed them to bear testimony of what they had seen and felt. Their testimonies are found at the front of the Book of Mormon. In later years, all three of these men would leave the Church and break their association with Joseph Smith. However, Moroni's visit and instructions had such a profound impact on each of these men that they never denied their testimonies. The fact that they never denied their testimony is truly the exceptional strength of their witness.

Oliver Cowdery was Joseph Smith's close associate during the Restoration. He was often with Joseph when angels appeared. After Oliver separated from the Church, he talked to Jacob Gates, a Mormon leader and member of the first seven presidents of the Seventy, about the appearance of the angel Moroni. The meeting took place in Richmond, Missouri, after Oliver had come back into the Church. Elder Gates's son tells the account:

> My father, Jacob Gates, while on his way to England, in 1849, stopped at the town of Richmond, where lived at that time Oliver Cowdery. Hearing that Oliver was in poor health, and wishing to renew old acquaintance, as they had been friends in earlier days, father called on him at his home. Their conversation, during the visit drifted to early Church history, and to their mutual experiences during the troublous times in Missouri and Illinois. Finally father put this question to him: "Oliver," said he, "I want you to tell me the whole truth about your testimony concerning the Book of Mormon—the testimony sent forth to the world over your signature and found in the front of that book. Was your testimony based on a dream, was it the imagination of your mind, was it an illusion, a myth—tell me truthfully?"
>
> To question him thus seemed to touch Oliver very deeply. He answered not a word, but arose from his easy chair, went to the book case, took down a Book of Mormon of the first edition, turned to the testimony of the Three Witnesses, and read in the most solemn manner the words to which he had subscribed his name, nearly twenty years before. Facing my father, he said: "Jacob, I want you to remember what I say to you. I am a dying man, and what would it profit me to tell you a lie? I know," said he, "that this Book of Mormon was translated by the gift and power of God. My eyes saw, my ears heard, and my understanding was touched, and I know that whereof I testified is true. It was no dream, no vain imagination of the mind—it was real."
>
> Then father asked him about the angel under whose hands he received the priesthood, to which he made answer thus: "Jacob, I felt the hand of the angel on my head as plainly as I could feel yours, and could hear his voice as I now hear yours."

> Then father asked this question: "If all that you tell me is true, why did you leave the Church?" Oliver made only this explanation; said he: "When I left the Church, I felt wicked, I felt like shedding blood, but I have got all over that now."[75]

Oliver traveled to Winter Quarters, Nebraska, where he asked to be reunited with the Church. On November 12, 1848, Oliver was rebaptized into the Church in Iowa. He never joined the Saints in Salt Lake but died March 3, 1850, at the age of 43 in Richmond, Missouri.

Another whole book could be written on just the visits from angels that Joseph Smith had during the time of the Restoration. These visits instructed and taught Joseph about the organization of the Church. They were also sent to celebrate this great time in which we live. The Doctrine and Covenant gave a partial list of those that came to teach and rejoice.

> Now, what do we hear in the gospel which we have received? A voice of gladness! . . .
>
> Glad tidings from Cumorah! Moroni, an angel from heaven, declaring the fulfilment of the prophets. . . . A voice of the Lord in the wilderness of Fayette, Seneca county, declaring the three witnesses to bear record of the book! The voice of Michael on the banks of the Susquehanna. . . . The voice of Peter, James, and John in the wilderness between Harmony, Susquehanna county, and Colesville . . . declaring themselves as possessing the keys of the kingdom, and of the dispensation of the fulness of times!
>
> And again, the voice of God. . . . And the voice of Michael, the archangel; the voice of Gabriel, and of Raphael, and of divers angels, from Michael or Adam down to the present time, all declaring their dispensation, their rights, their keys, their honors, their majesty and glory, and the power of their priesthood; giving line upon line, precept upon precept; here a little, and there a little; giving us consolation by holding forth that which is to come, confirming our hope. (D&C 128:19–21)

Joseph was well instructed. When I read things that Joseph Smith has written, I am amazed at his command of the language and his profound teachings. Joseph with his third grade education was taught well by these prophet angels. These teaching angels had a quick learner and a fresh mind to work with. Joseph taught that if you could "gaze into heaven five minutes, you would know more than you would by reading all that ever was written on the subject."[76]

Frederick William Hurst was working as a gold miner in Australia when he first heard Latter-day Saint missionaries preach the restored gospel. He and his brother Charles were baptized on January 1854. He tried to help his other family members become converted, but they rejected him and the truths he taught.

Frederick settled in Salt Lake City four years after joining the Church, and he served faithfully as a missionary in several different countries. He also worked as a painter in the Salt Lake Temple.

One of Frederick William Hurst's brothers had passed away but wanted his temple work done. When Frederick's deceased brother, Alfred, appeared to him, he had some specific instruction for his brother. In one of his final journal entries, Frederick wrote,

> Along about the 1st of March, 1893, I found myself alone in the dining room, all had gone to bed. I was sitting at the table when to my great surprise my elder brother Alfred walked in and sat down opposite me at the table and smiled. I said to him (he looked so natural): "When did you arrive in Utah?"
>
> He said: "I have just come from the Spirit World, this is not my body that you see, it is lying in the tomb. I want to tell you that when you were on your mission you told me many things about the Gospel, and the hereafter, and about the Spirit World being as real and tangible as the earth. I could not believe you, but when I died and went there and saw for myself I realized that you had told the truth. I attended the Mormon meetings." He raised his hand and said with much warmth: "I believe in the Lord Jesus Christ with all my heart. I believe in faith, and repentance and baptism for the remission of sins, but that is as far as I can go. I look to you to do the work for me in the temple. . . . You are watched closely. . . . We are all looking to you as our head in this great work. I want to tell you that there are a great many spirits who weep and mourn because they have relatives in the Church here who are careless and are doing nothing for them."[77]

We may have relatives that weep and mourn because we are not doing the family history research and temple work that they need. It shouldn't take a visit from an angel to teach us what prophets have been instructing us to do since the Church was organized.

I will use a full chapter for modern day examples of angels teaching and instructing. When an angel teaches and instructs us it is usually a call for us to act.

Chapter 8

When Angels Teach or Instruct, It Is a Call for Us to Act

An angel—a heavenly messenger sent for a purpose—is not going to visit us to merely satisfy our curiosity. When we receive a message, it is for a reason. There is something to be done!

Joseph Fielding Smith said, "It is contrary to the law of God for the heavens to be opened and messengers to come and do anything for man that man can do for himself."[78] What would be the point of teaching or instructing a person if they will not act on the knowledge received? I have students fall asleep in my classes. Sometime they fall asleep because they were up most of the night doing homework. Sometimes they are sick and just can't miss school, so they try to make it through the day. But when a student attends day after day and puts their head down before class even starts, I know there is a problem.

President Dieter F. Uchtdorf, in April conference 2014, gave a talk called "Are You Sleeping through the Restoration?" He gave three reasons why people don't act. The first reason was selfishness or the "What's in it for me?" The second reason was addictions and the third reason was competing priorities. He asks us this question, "Will we be able to say that we rolled up our sleeves and labored with all our heart, might, mind, and strength? Or will we have to admit that our role was mostly that of an observer?"[79]

He was not referring to angel's visits or promptings, but if we are blessed with that experience it will be to inspire us to roll up our sleeves and get to work. President Henry B. Eyring said, "When the Spirit confirms eternal truth, there is always something to be done about it."[80] If angels are agents for the Holy Ghost, we should expect that we need to act on truth given by them. Just as the examples in the previous chapter demonstrated that actions were required when angels taught and instructed in the scriptures and in early Church history, so it is with us today.

Hearts and lives can be changed by the impact of angelic visits. There are those that make a complete change in their lives after encountering an angel as did Paul, Alma the Younger, and Amulek. A person with a workable, humble heart emerges a better person, more dedicated to doing God's work. Those with hard hearts like Laman and Lemuel do not change. Laman and Lemuel saw an angel and it didn't have much of an impact on their stubborn nature. Edifying experiences should require some kind of action on our part.

I will share some accounts of angels teaching or instructing us today. I will start out with an experience I had.

I know it would be a huge stretch to say angels control computers, but that is how I felt one day after working in the stake family history center. I was a stake consultant and we had set a goal for our stake to complete five generations of their family history. We hoped that the stake would complete all the temple work for those five generations.

I had spent four hours doing my shift and stayed past the time when I should have left, trying to clear some final names for ordinance work in the temple. I was pleased with my efforts and as I pushed the button to save to disk, the computer froze. I was livid. I was afraid that all my hours of work were wasted. I went home grumbling under my breath how dumb computers were and wishing deep inside I could throw the computer at the wall and smash it.

Several weeks later I had time to return to the stake family history center. Because I worked in the center, I had a key. I left my husband watching the children and explained it could take me several hours to recreate what was previously lost.

I got right to work and everything seemed to be going great. It was quiet and no one was in the building. I got to a name, Margaret Ann Richey. I distinctly remembered passing over that name and thinking she didn't need any other ordinances. I heard a voice say, "Don't you forget me too!" Who was this Margaret Ann Richey? I quickly switched on some of the other computers and started looking up information on the name. Margaret had been married civilly to her husband, Jens "J" Hansen in 1886. Margaret had died a year later. Two years later, in 1888, her husband, Jens, married her sister, Johanna Jeannette Richey. On the day Jens and Johanna were married and sealed in the temple, someone had done Margaret's endowment work. Margaret had never been sealed to her husband, Jens.

That evening I knew why I needed to spend several more hours redoing my work. Weeks before I had skimmed over her name without a second thought. She had been waiting for 108 years for someone to catch the fact that she needed to be sealed. On September 13, 1994, my husband and I knelt across the altar at the Provo temple and did the work Margaret had personally requested. I sensed that her long wait was finally over. I have no doubt that she was there that evening.

Family history work is a call to action. I don't know of a work that will bring you closer to the world of spirits than family history and temple work. We have loved ones that have waited for many years for their work to be done. As the missionary work here is hastening, that same hastening is being experienced in the world of spirits. With that increased effort there may be times when those waiting will have to push us in the right direction. The youth of the Church have come prepared to hasten not only missionary work but family history work.

Elder Quentin L. Cook put some of the responsibility for this work on the shoulders of the youth of the Church.

> The leadership of the Church has issued a clarion call to the rising generation to lead the way in the use of technology to experience the spirit of Elijah, to search out their ancestors, and to perform temple ordinances for them. Much of the heavy lifting in hastening the

> work of salvation for both the living and the dead will be done by you young people.
>
> If the youth in each ward will not only go to the temple and do baptisms for their dead but also work with their families and other ward members to provide the family names for the ordinance work they perform, both they and the Church will be greatly blessed. *Don't underestimate the influence of the deceased in assisting your efforts* and the joy of ultimately meeting those you serve. The eternally significant blessing of uniting our own families is almost beyond comprehension.[81]

The youth of this Church certainly have a knowledge of the operation of electronic devices enabling them to do this work for those on the other side of the veil.

The veil is very thin as we labor to perform work for our loved ones as President Packer taught us after the death of A. Theodore Tuttle:

> The more I have to do with genealogical work, the more difficulty I have with that word dead. I know of no adequate substitute. I suppose departed would suit me as well as any. I have had too many sacred experiences, of the kind of which we never speak lightly, to feel that the word dead describes those who have gone beyond the veil.
>
> Temple and genealogy work are visible testimonies of our belief in the resurrection and Atonement of the Lord Jesus Christ. . . .
>
> Now what of Brother Tuttle or of his family? I remind you that it is a veil, not a wall, which separates us from the spirit world. He kept his covenants. Veils can become thin, even parted. We are not left to do this work alone.
>
> They who have preceded us in this work and our forebears there, on occasion, are very close to us. I have a testimony of this work; it is a supernal work in the Church. I am a witness that those who go beyond the veil yet live and minister here, to the end that this work might be completed.[82]

Temple and family history work is a two-edged sword. It blesses those that have gone on before us but it equally blesses us. If you want to brush close to the spirit world and the angels, do family history work.

Elder Russell M. Nelson said, "While temple and family history work has the power to bless those beyond the veil, it has an equal power to bless the living. It has a refining influence on those who are engaged in it. They are literally helping to exalt their families."[83]

The next several stories involve angels that instruct others to act. Elder Quentin L. Cook shared an experience of a sister hearing the voice of someone she was doing temple work for.

> One faithful sister shared a special spiritual experience in the Salt Lake Temple. While in the confirmation room, after a vicarious confirmation ordinance was pronounced, she heard, "And the prisoner shall go free!" She felt a great sense of urgency for those who were waiting for their baptismal and confirmation work. Upon returning home, she searched the scriptures for the phrase she had heard. She found Joseph Smith's declaration in section 128 of the Doctrine and Covenants: "Let your hearts rejoice, and be exceedingly glad. Let the earth break forth into singing. Let the dead speak forth anthems of eternal praise to the King Immanuel, who hath ordained, before the world was, that which would enable us to redeem them out of their prison; for the prisoners shall go free."[84]

This account makes you wonder how many of our families members are waiting to be freed. As members of this Church, we are indebted to those that have caught the vision of this labor. They serve all of us as they extract names, link families, and provide work to be done in the temples.

The *Ensign* shared an account of a man named Milton E. Page who played a part in forty-two members of his family getting their temple work done. The fascinating part of the account was that Milton E. Page had died prior to his role in this story.

As it often happens in family history research, there is a line with very limited information available. This article is the account of such a line. Merle (the author) tells of Albert Page (his great-great-grandfather). He was born in Chicago but moved to Mexico after marrying a Spanish girl and fearing repercussions from his wealthy family.

They had eight children before Albert died. His wife burned all the documents that tied her children to the Chicago family to avoid the possibility that his family might try to take the children away.

This created a difficulty in finding information about the

Chicago family. Merle's mother and aunts searched to find connections without success. Merle's mother had dreams about a " 'fine-looking gentleman' who would appear and look at her with a smile as if he were waiting for something."[85] These dreams went on for years until Merle stepped in and decided to help look for these missing relatives. Merle looked for the wealthy Chicago father, who they thought was named Edgar Page. He could not find him at the family history center or at the university library (looking through old Chicago phone books).

After fasting, Merle returned to the family history center. Searching census records, he received the M–Z film of one instead of his intended A–L. Looking through it anyway, Merle found a Milton E. Page whose children's names matched up with those of his grandmother's siblings. He found a phone number for this person and when he called the number, an elderly lady answered. Milton E. Page Jr. had had been her father. Merle asked her to tell him about her grandfather. In the course of their conversation, she mentioned one uncle had gone to Mexico.

Realizing the likelihood of their being related, Merle cried and told her that her uncle was his great-grandfather. She was surprised but agreed to an arranged visit with him, his wife, mother, and daughter.

While hesitant at first, the elderly lady finally showed Merle and his family her family Bible during their visit. Merle said, "As I opened the family Bible, a picture fell out and my mother picked it up. She immediately began to sob. It was the man in her dreams: my great-great-grandfather Milton Edwin Page, Albert's father.

With the documentation from the family Bible, we were able to go to the Ogden Utah Temple and complete the ordinances for 42 people."[85]

Milton's angelic visits were the catalyst for this family finding their lost family line.

These visits from Milton Page were not to satisfy the mother's curiosity. There was work that needed to be done. Many of us have felt that nagging feeling that we needed to do something for our family members that have passed on. That nagging feeling has a name, the spirit of Elijah. Ann describes so well what it feels like in the following story.

Ann Lewis, an avid family history researcher, wrote in her journal and explained the feelings she experienced from spirits on the other side waiting for their work to be done.

> Wednesday 14 October 2009, 3:45 p.m. Taking Down the Puzzle. I just pushed all the pieces of the CMS puzzle off the dining room table and into the box. It's been sitting there, unfinished since December, when the kids were home from school. That puzzle has been a reminder to me all these months of what is important.
>
> A few days before school let out for Christmas vacation, I was knee deep in family history work, wondering how my Kindred Dead would leave me alone long enough to get through Christmas as a proper Mom. I was really worried—they seldom give me a break. But I had shopping to do, gifts to wrap, and cookies to bake—and the kids would be home from school soon.
>
> So I prayed that I would be able to focus on them and function well among the living while they were home. The day school let out, my Kindred Dead went away. Just like that, they went away. No hovering, no prompting, no presence. I felt like I needed to keep looking around me to find them. I worried about where they had gone. I hesitatingly closed my computer and got out the wrapping paper, the flour, sugar, and sprinkles, and I spent time shopping with the kids. It was fun. It was relaxing. I slept at night instead of thinking about finding people I didn't know. And then I started a puzzle. Santa in his workshop—1500 pieces. It would take hours. And while Christmas music filled our home and cookies baked, and visitors dropped by, I filled in spare moments putting pieces in the puzzle. It was a hard one. I often sat down at that dining room table determined to find "just 3 more pieces" but then I stayed for a half an hour or maybe even an hour. Slowly the picture on the box came together in the pieces on the table. After finishing the edges. Santa's red suit came next, then parts of his workshop and toys came together. Aaron often joined me and others were in and out of the room, enjoying the tree and practicing Christmas music on the piano.
>
> It was a wonderful holiday. Peaceful. Relaxing, Filled with family, friends, good food, and warmth. The puzzle continued to come together. I worked on it after Christmas while the room was

scattered with Christmas debris until New Year's Day while eating New Year's donuts.

It was in that week after Christmas that They came back. My Dead People. I think it was about the time the kids didn't need me anymore—they were off skiing with friends and doing their things, leaving John and me home alone, and then school started. And when They came back, They came back to stay. And they've been here ever since.

So today I took the puzzle down. Unfinished. Sadye messed it all up last week, and it didn't bother me too much, because I knew I'd never finish it, not unless They went away again. I've got a bigger puzzle to work on now. I can't see the whole picture yet, but I know what it is: a picture of our Family.

This story demonstrates how badly those on the other side want their temple work done. Ann Lewis could not rest. Those angels or spirits had the faith and trust that she would follow through with promptings given.

These angels from the world of spirits also come to nonmembers requesting that their work be done. I asked a friend of ours to share her conversion story with me for this book. Mary was not a member of the Church when she married Dennis. Dennis was not active in the Church when this experience occurred. Mary had been talking to the missionaries since she only knew a little bit about the Church. This is her conversion story.

I [Mary] had a very dear friend and colleague, Sue. I loved her dearly, but she suddenly passed away from a heart attack. My husband, Dennis, and I were at Lake Powell when I got the word that Sue had passed away. After a very emotional discussion with Sue's husband by cell phone, Dennis and I were driving back to our lodging when I heard this very loud voice in my head that said "Sue needs to be baptized!" I was crying and very emotional and couldn't understand why that thought had popped into my head at that moment. Then again, a second time, the same very loud voice said to me "Sue needs to be baptized!"

I turned to Dennis with tears running down my face and said, "I keep hearing this voice that says, 'Sue needs to be baptized.' I don't understand." He looked at me and said, "I think the only way Sue is going to get baptized is if you get baptized and you do the work for her." Dennis had been less active for many years and had started his own journey back to the Church a few months earlier, and I had been moving closer to seriously considering joining the Church. I truly believe that the Lord used this loss to personally talk to me to let me know it was time—even though I still had many questions unanswered. Within a few weeks, Dennis had become active again, I had quickly gone back through the discussions, and Dennis baptized me.

A few months after that, I had dinner with Sue's husband (he was a dear friend too) and was prompted while we were at dinner to tell him about my experience at Lake Powell. Neither he nor Sue was religious. They were wonderful, loving, kind, generous people but didn't believe in an afterlife. He was deeply touched by my story. I was bold enough to explain about baptisms for the dead and told him I'd be back in a year to ask him if I could be baptized for Sue. He told me he'd think about it. I had dinner several other times with him over the next year. After a year had gone by, we were together again and I asked him if he'd thought about my desire to be baptized for Sue. He said he had and had decided the answer was no. I asked him why and he said that if there was a God, someone like Sue clearly would be with him now. To be honest, I had, and still have, a hard time arguing with that. She was the most wonderful person I'd ever known. He then asked me why I wanted to do this and I told him Sue had given me so much over the years this was one thing that I wanted to give to her—that she could accept it or not on the other side—but I deeply wanted to give her this choice. With that he said his answer was easy—he knew if Sue was sitting here she'd say 'yes,' because it was important to me. So I was able to be baptized for Sue and do all of her temple work. It's been a most wonderful experience for me and I pray she's accepted the work on the other side.

It was an amazing experience for Dennis and me. The Spirit has never been stronger for me than at that moment at Lake Powell. I figured I truly had a "broken heart and contrite spirit" at that moment and He took the opportunity to speak to me strongly and lovingly to pull me into His fold.

What an amazing Heavenly Father we have and what love He has for us.

When we see or hear from messengers or the Holy Ghost, we are edified, uplifted, enlightened, informed, and/or challenged to act. There may be few words used when angels communicate but there are a multitude of insights and feelings expressed. Mary heard, "Sue needs to be baptized." Ann felt the urgency of many spirits waiting. Milton E. Page made several appearances. The faithful sister heard a scripture phrase quoted, "And the prisoner shall go free." I heard, "Don't you forget me too." All of these were simple phrases that have motivated the listeners to act.

The same advice would hold true with the communication we receive from angels. These examples shared all demonstrated our need to do something.

President Wilford Woodruff had a call to action. The signers of the Declaration of Independence came to him, asking him to do their temple work. Might not our departed family members that have not been blessed by the ordinances of the temple also be calling after us?

> I feel to say little else to the Latter-day Saints wherever and whenever I have the opportunity of speaking to them, than to call upon them to build these temples now under way, to hurry them up to completion. The dead will be after you; they will seek after you as they have after us in St. George. They called upon us, knowing that we held the keys and power to redeem them.
>
> I will here say, before closing, that two weeks before I left St. George, the spirits of the dead gathered round me, wanting to know why we did not redeem them. Said they, "You have had the use of the Endowment House for a number of years, and yet nothing has ever been done for us. We laid the foundation of the government you now enjoy, and we never apostatized from it; but we remained true to it and were faithful to God." These were the signers of the Declaration of Independence, and they waited on me for two days and two nights. I thought it very singular that notwithstanding so much work had been done, and yet nothing had been done for them. The thought never entered my heart—from the fact, I suppose, that heretofore our minds were reaching after out more immediate friends and relatives. I straightway went into the baptismal font and called upon Brother McAllister to baptize me for the signers of the Declaration of Independence and fifty other eminent men, making one hundred in all, including, John Wesley, Columbus, and others. I then baptized him for every president of the United States except three; and when their cause is just somebody will do the work for them."[86]

If the Declaration of Independence was inspired by God as we claim, then the men who received and acted upon that inspiration deserved every right to receive their blessings through the ordinances of the temple. They deserved this right, especially when you consider that it was their sacrifice that made it possible to have a country where the gospel could be restored.

This next account was given by President Heber J. Grant. The following angelic messenger had to give repeated requests to a friend until her friend followed through with her desire to be married and sealed. The sister delivering the message needed a lot of prodding to convince her to act.

> There was three young men who were as intimate, I think, as any three young men who ever lived could be. They were Heber J. Grant, Feramorz L. Young and Richard W. Young. Feramorz L. Young had been in the East and had been graduated with honors from the Troy Polytechnic Institute, then went on a mission to Mexico, where he died and was buried in the Gulf of Mexico. It always seemed to me a strange thing that a boy with all the education he had, who had made a wonderful success should be taken from us. . . . He had to fight for the Church and its doctrines all the time he was in the East. . . .
>
> I thought that with his faith and knowledge, and with all the information he had gained, it was too bad he had to lay down his life while in the Lord's service. . . .
>
> I do not think that Fera Young in his life ever listened to an unclean story. If anyone started to tell such a story, he would excuse himself and walk away. I never heard an unchaste word uttered by him. If there ever was a clean, sweet, absolutely pure young man upon the earth, he was that young man.
>
> [When] he died, his mother said she could not remember a word or thought or act of his life that would bring her the least sorrow or uneasiness. There is many a mother perhaps who might say such a thing of her son, but usually if the man who without exception was the most intimate friend of that son from his boyhood up to the time of his death should tell everything he knew of him, the mother could not say that. My mother could not say that of me, if others told her what I did as a youngster, but I could say it of Feramorz Young.
>
> What in the providence of the Lord is the result? . . . A woman came to Sister Young, his mother, with photographs of one of this lady's near and dear friends, a very beautiful women, and said: "Now,

Mrs. Young, I do not believe a thing of what I'm going to tell you. This girl friend of mine was one of the noblest, finest, choicest kind of girls and young women that ever lived. She has come to me in this city of Salt Lake on three separate occasions at night in dreams, and has given me this information: the date of her birth, the date of her death, and all this is necessary, she says, for a record in the temple: and she has told me that your son, Feramorz L. Young, has converted her, and that in addition to converting her he has proposed marriage to her." [She has said to me] 'I want you to go to Mrs. Young and give her this information and vouch for my honesty, virtue, integrity and upright life, and have the work done for me and have me married for eternity to her son, Feramorz L. Young.' "

This women who visited Mrs. Young said: "I do not believe a word of it, but the last time this friend of mine came—which was the third time—she said, 'There is nobody in Salt Lake City who knows me and can vouch for me except you. You are the only individual that I know in Salt Lake City.' " She said further to Mrs. Young: "I can furnish you any references you may wish regarding my character, from the place where I formerly lived. The last time this young woman came to me she said, 'You might just as well go to Mrs. Young and give her this information, because I am going to come, and come, and come, until you do it.' " And the woman continued, "I just cannot bear to have her come again; it is so uncanny, and I do not believe a thing of it."

This beautiful girl was sealed to Brother Young, and I am convinced that my dear friend lost nothing by dying in his youth.[87]

An angel giving instructions can be very persistent as the above account emphasizes. You can see that there could be an entire book written on angels/spirits requesting or desiring that their temple work be done. I have never felt the veil as thin as when I worked in our stake family history center. Patrons on a daily basis seemed to have those "aha" moments when things would just come together. This story shows the great push that is happening on the other side of the veil.

In May 1884, Bishop Henry Ballard of the Logan Second Ward was signing temple recommends at his home. Henry's nine-year-old daughter, who was talking with friends on the sidewalk near her home, saw two elderly men approaching. They called to her, handed her a newspaper, and told her to take it to her father.

> The girl did as she was asked. Bishop Ballard saw that the paper, the Newbury Weekly News, published in England, contained the names of more than 60 of his and his father's acquaintances, along with genealogical information. This newspaper, dated 15 May 1884, had been given to him only three days after it was printed. In a time long before air transportation, when mail took several weeks to get from England to western America, this was a miracle.
>
> The next day, Bishop Ballard took the newspaper to the temple and told the story of its arrival to Marriner W. Merrill, the temple president. President Merrill declared, 'Brother Ballard, someone on the other side is anxious for their work to be done and they knew that you would do it if this paper got into your hands.' This newspaper is preserved in the Church Historical Library in Salt Lake City, Utah.[88]

There is no doubt that angels teach and instruct us as they have in the past. In the Washington, DC, temple a member of the temple presidency use to greet each group before their session. One morning, President Colton made this statement, "Just like converts to the Church never forget the name of their missionary that brought the gospel into their life, so those in the spirit world will not forget those that perform the saving ordinances for them in the temple." My hope is that if our ears are tuned and we hear their instructions and pleadings that we may act or they may find someone else that will act.

Chapter 9

Angels Prophesy of Things to Come

"The revelations of God which shall come hereafter by the gift and power of the Holy Ghost, the voice of God, or the ministering of angels" (D&C 20:35; emphasis added).

Angels are sent to prophesy of things to come. An excellent example of an angel prophesying of future events is found in 1 Nephi chapters 11 through 15. Nephi was shown the Savior's ministry, baptism, and crucifixion. He was shown the land of promise and coming of Jesus Christ. An angel showed Nephi the interpretation of the dream his father had about the Tree of Life and what that dream meant to all of us. He was shown the colonizing of America, the latter-day scriptures, the Bible, and the reaction to latter-day scriptures. Nephi understood that the Gentiles would bring the gospel to Lehi's descendants. He saw the same revelation given to John the Revelator and he was told not to write any portion of the vision. Nephi was told that the one assigned to write this portion of the vision would be one of the twelve Apostles called John.

Furthermore, Samuel the Lamanite was told by an angel of specific signs that would accompany the birth and death of the Savior. "An angel of the Lord hath declared it unto me, and he did bring glad tidings to my soul" (Helaman 13:7). He prophesied that at the birth of Christ there would be "a new star arise, such an one as ye never have beheld" (Helaman 14:5), and "one day and a night and a day, as if it were one day and there were no night" (Helaman 14:4).

Samuel then gave a sign of the Savior's death, "the sun shall be darkened and refuse to give his light unto you; and also the moon and the stars; and there shall be no light upon the face of this land, even from the time that he shall suffer death, for the space of three days, to the time that he shall rise again from the dead" (Helaman 14:20).

In the book of Judges in the Old Testament, an angel rebukes Israel for not serving the Lord as they had previously covenanted that they would do. The Lord had promised to drive out the inhabitants of the land if the Israelites would remove the pagan altars. The angel prophesied that because "ye have not obeyed my voice. . . . I will not drive them out from before you; but they shall be as thorns in your sides, and their gods shall be a snare unto you" (Judges 2:2–3). This prophecy was fulfilled. The Israelites struggled with idol worship until they were destroyed or finally captured.

In the early days of the Restoration, the angel Moroni appeared to Joseph Smith in his room and taught him from the scriptures, prophesying that these prophecies of the Bible were about to come to pass.

> He also quoted the second chapter of Joel, from the twenty-eighth verse to the last. He also said that this *was not yet fulfilled*, but was soon to be. And he further stated that the fulness of the Gentiles was soon to come in. He quoted many other passages of scripture, and offered many explanations which cannot be mentioned here. (Joseph Smith—History 1:41; emphasis added)

We live in an exciting time in the history of the world while these prophecies unfold and we witness visions that prophets have seen for centuries. In the verse above, Moroni quoted Joel, saying that Joel's prophecy was not yet fulfilled but that it would come to pass shortly. Our ears should have pricked up when President Gordon B. Hinckley made this statement, "The vision of Joel has been fulfilled."[89] I will let you look up in scripture what Joel saw that Moroni said would shortly come to pass and that President Hinckley stated has occurred.

It is obvious from these examples that angels are often sent to tell mortal men what is to happen or what will eventually transpire.

Are we aware that angels come to the "common members" as well as to prophets? Angels appear to prophets to declare the truth to all the world. However, angels appear to individuals for special messages for them only. If angels appear to someone other than the prophet, that message is private, for that individual and not for the Church as a whole. Angels can be sent to prophesy of events that will transpire in our own lives. The following story is a very special example in my family of angels prophesying of things to come:

My brother and sister-in-law were married for five years and desperately wanted children. They watched while friends and family were blessed with children. Each baby blessing and announcement silently added salt to their wounded hearts. The story that follows really didn't bring comfort at first and it nearly seemed a cruel reminder that they were childless. This is their story. Karen, my sister-in-law, wrote this account in April 1982.

> One Sunday our Bishop asked us to come to his office after Sunday school. As we sat down he seemed very ill at ease and nervous. He said he had something to tell us but before he did he wanted us to know he was not a visionary man and had never had such an experience before. For several weeks he had tried to ignore and forget what had happened, but he couldn't get it off his mind. He finally confided in his counselors and they felt the only way he would feel peace of mind would be to tell us what had happened. There we sat, completely puzzled as he related this story.
>
> Several weeks earlier he had been sitting in his office at church, working, when he sensed someone in the room. He glanced up and saw 5 children standing before him. He did not recognize them and thought they might be from another ward. He said, "Who are you—who do you belong to?" One of the children answered, "We are the Larsen children!" Our Bishop then said, "that can't be, the Larsen's' don't have any children!" The child then said, "We have not been born, the time is not right for us to come to earth yet!"
>
> You can imagine us going home full of joy and hope, but we didn't. In fact Jeff and I hardly spoke about it at all and we promptly forgot the incident. I guess I was so bitter and emotionally low that I really didn't listen. I remember thinking how could this be. I've been going to infertility specialists for years to no avail, if you adopted children the most you can adopt is 2, and even if I were to become

pregnant I'm too old to have that many children now. I can truthfully say I completely forgot the incident for years.

[Jeff and Karen were able to adopt a little girl who they named Amber in Feb. of 1975. Shortly after adopting Amber, Karen got pregnant and delivered their second child in April 1976.]

Then, finally, when I was in the hospital having Jaron, our third child, I remember telling my roommate that I have 3 children and the oldest was 2. All of a sudden everything came rushing back to me and I thought, it is possible! I really could have 5 children!

Since that time this incident has gained significant meaning for me. But the spiritual feelings did not come all at once. At one time I could have explained everything away by logic and chance, but not now.

It is interesting to think that for years I knew exactly when I was ovulating and knew everything was functioning normally. The doctors were all puzzled and couldn't understand why I wasn't pregnant. I realize emotions do play a part, but it is significant to note that after Amber, our adopted daughter, came to us, I became pregnant the very first month we tried, and every time thereafter! We believe that regardless of the special circumstances bringing Amber to us, she was meant to be our first child and is as much a part of our eternal family as her biological brothers and sister.

Our Bishop did not take this experience lightly. Years later, after we had moved and lost track of Bishop Merrill, he became acquainted with a friend of ours who had also served as bishop. In discussing their experiences as bishops he mentioned that this was one of the most spiritual experiences he had ever had!

With the wisdom of a few years, we have learned several lessons from this experience. The first lesson, which many people have trouble learning, is to accept the Lord's timetable. How many times do we pray and are so impatient, we want action or answers immediately. In our imperfect logic we can see no reason why we should be denied the blessings we seek. Why should we be denied the privilege of bearing children when many people prevent children, abort children, or abuse children? And now, with the passage of time, I realize what a blessing Amber has been to us. We have grown so much together. Life without her in our family is unthinkable.

Another important lesson I've learned is the realization that we must be prepared to receive counsel or answers to our prayers. Going through the mechanics of problem solving and asking the Lord if a decision is the right one, or even having a spiritual experience is not enough. One must be spiritually ready for an answer; that means being in tune and perceptive enough to comprehend the wisdom of answers we receive, and humble enough to accept what we can't understand. It is interesting to note that the same experience that at one time provokes feelings of doubt and resentment, yet with a few years behind us, we can learn valuable lessons and recognize the wisdom gained from the same experience.

And now for the climax of this letter—It is with great anticipation that we announce the fulfillment of the revelation with number 5 due in November!!! We will have 5 children in 7 calendar years! Whew! Knowing my own strength and limitations and feeling strongly about being able to provide each child with an abundance of emotional support, time, and love, we will have to rely heavily on the Lord's judgment and depend on Him for strength and guidance.

When angels prophesy, the acceptance of their message depends on our own spiritual preparation. This experience produced resentment that turned to honor and praise. It is hard to get excited about a prophecy when you can't see how it could possibly happen. Jeff and Karen's bishop was right. They do have five children.

It would be interesting to know the exact day you would die. This is precisely what happened to President Ezra Taft Benson's mother-in-law. Donald W. Perry, who was a professor of the Hebrew Bible at Brigham Young University, related this account.

President Ezra Taft Benson "recounted an eternal love story of his wife's parents. His father-in-law, Carl Christian Amussen, a convert from Denmark, was a watchmaker and jeweler in Utah. He passed away in 1902, leaving his wife, Barbara, a widow for forty years.

In 1942, the deceased Carl came to his wife to inform her of her approaching death. What a great blessing it was for her to see her eternal companion for the first time in so many years. Carl appeared to Barbara and informed her that she would pass away on the following Thursday. Barbara had no doubt that her husband had appeared to her, nor did she doubt that she only had less than a week to live; in fact she began to make concrete plans for her death. On Sunday at church, she bore her testimony and bid the ward members good-bye. During the coming days she withdrew her savings from the bank, ordered her casket from a local mortuary, paid her bills, and even had the power and water turned off at her home. Then she went to her daughter Mabel's home to await her passing.

> President Benson concluded:
>
> 'On the day of her passing, Mabel came into the room where her mother was reclining on the bed. Her mother said, "Mabel, I feel a little bit drowsy. I feel I will go to sleep. Do not disturb me if I sleep until the eventide."
>
> Those were her last words and she peacefully passed away.'"[90]

Barbara did not doubt the delivered prophecy by her belated husband. Because of her great faith she acted on the words he conveyed and was prepared to greet him.

As mentioned in an earlier chapter, we can also serve as angels. Patriarchs of the Church serve in the position of angels who deliver personal prophecy. They are agents of the Lord, who speak by the power of the Holy Ghost and deliver the Lord's admonitions to individuals that are worthy and wanting to receive the Lord's counsel. These holy men of God deliver prophecies of our potentialities. Patriarchs are a good example of the relationship with divine angels and our lives. Angels are agents of the Lord, who speak by the power of the Holy Ghost and deliver His blessings to us.

At one point in my life, through a manifestation of the Spirit, I was shown the joy that would occur in my life when all my children were active and partakers of God's glorious plan. When our children wander from the truth, there is an indescribable pain that really never goes away. I have never lost a child of my own and had to stand by the coffin and say my final good-bye. I know this shows my lack of understanding and I apologize to those that have suffered from that pain. Yet, I can't imagine the pain is any more intense than watching your child die spiritually in front of you and you are helpless to save them. The vision that I beheld of my own family brought great comfort as I was shown what could be. The joy was so powerful that for that moment I could no longer feel the pain, the sorrow, and heartache that filled my heart with a wayward child. The pain was swallowed up in the joy that I felt. I knew that whatever it took to get to that moment, it would be insignificant in comparison to the joy I felt. That small glimpse has made the waiting for eternal promises bearable. I liked the way Sister Linda S. Reeves, second counselor in the Relief Society general presidency, expressed this same idea in the October 2015 women's conference.

Sister Reeves said, "I do not know why we have the many trials that we have, but it is my personal feeling that the reward is so great, so eternal and everlasting, so joyful and beyond our understanding that in that day of reward, we may feel to say to our merciful, loving Father, 'Was that *all* that was required?' "[91]

Amaleki reminds us "to come unto God, the Holy One of Israel, and believe in prophesying, and in revelations, and in the ministering of angels" (Omni 1:25). Don't allow unbelief to rob us of the help the Lord is willing to give us. Elder Mark E. Petersen said, "In these modern times the very mention of angels brings scoffs and scorn from some critical listeners who say that angelic ministrations are a thing of the past, if they actually ever did occur. . . . Because the Lord desires to save mankind, even until the end, He revealed to John the Revelator that in the latter days angels would again fly through the midst of heaven as emissaries of the Almighty."[92]

I am grateful for the reassurance that I am not alone. God's promises and prophecies will be fulfilled. As mentioned earlier, "And the office of their ministry is to . . . fulfil and to do the work of the covenants of the Father, which he hath made unto the children of men" (Moroni 7:31).

Chapter 10

Angels Provide Protection

The term guardian angel is probably the most common reference to angels. The term "guardian angel" is a term used when an angel protects us. There are countless stories of protecting angels. There could be and have been entire books about angels protecting individuals from harm. I am convinced that there are journals scattered throughout family closets telling of stories of angels protecting people.

Concerning protection by angels, James E. Talmage said,

> He is our Father; and He has greater affection than we can comprehend by father's love for His children. As a result of that great love, He has sent heavenly beings to watch over us and to guard us from the attacks of evil powers while we live on earth. Do we realize that in our daily walk and work we are not alone, but that angels attend us wherever our duty causes us to go? It is only when we stray into unholy places, only when we tread upon forbidden ground, that they leave us to ourselves; and then they watch us from the distance with sorrow and tears.[93]

Elder Talmage teaches us that we are not alone unless we stray into unholy places. It is an interesting thought that angels are weeping for us when we make wrong decisions. The book of Moses says the Lord also weeps for us: "And it came to pass that the God of heaven looked upon the residue of the people, and he wept" (Moses 7:28). Enoch witnessed God weeping and asked Him why He was weeping. The Lord answered, "Behold these thy brethren; they are the workmanship of mine own hands, and I gave unto them their knowledge, in the day I created them; and in the Garden of Eden, gave I unto man his agency" (Moses 7:32). When Enoch understood the Lord's sorrow he also wept: "He had bitterness of soul, and wept over his brethren" (Moses 7:44).

The sorrow for wickedness does not stop with angels, the Lord, or servants of the Lord, but extends to the earth itself:

> Enoch looked upon the earth; and he heard a voice from the bowels thereof, saying: Wo, wo is me, the mother of men; I am pained, I am weary, because of the wickedness of my children. When shall I rest, and be cleansed from the filthiness which is gone forth out of me? When will my Creator sanctify me that I may rest, and righteousness for a season abide upon my face?
>
> And when Enoch heard the earth mourn, he wept. (Moses 7:48–49)

I know from personal experience that tears are shed for our loved ones that stray. It is obvious that there are those beyond the veil besides those on earth that cry because of our actions. Sin doesn't affect just "me"; it affects all those that love "me."

A great account of an angel protecting the servants of the Lord is the story of Peter when he was thrown into prison by Herod. Peter was locked in prison and chained between two guards to prevent his escape.

> And when Herod would have brought him forth, the same night Peter was sleeping between two soldiers, bound with two chains: and the keepers before the door kept the prison.
>
> And, behold, the angel of the Lord came upon him, and a light shined in the prison: and he smote Peter on the side, and raised him up, saying, Arise up quickly. And his chains fell off from his hands.
>
> And the angel said unto him, Gird thyself, and bind on thy sandals. And so he did. And he saith unto him, Cast thy garment about thee, and follow me.
>
> And he went out, and followed him; and wist not that it was true which was done by the angel; but thought he saw a vision.
>
> When they were past the first and the second ward, they came unto the iron gate that leadeth unto the city; which opened to them

> of his own accord: and they went out, and passed on through one street; and forthwith the angel departed from him.
>
> And when Peter was come to himself, he said, Now I know of a surety, that the Lord hath sent his angel, and hath delivered me out of the hand of Herod, and from all the expectation of the people of the Jews. (Acts 12:6–11)

Truly, nothing is too hard for the Lord—or his angels. Chains, locked doors, and prison guards could not stop the angel of the Lord from delivering Peter. How would you explain to Herod how Peter got out?

One of my favorite stories of angels protecting the Lord's servant is the story of Daniel in the lion's den. Daniel found great favor with King Darius who in return made Daniel the first of his presidents. The other presidents were jealous of Daniel for being promoted above them. In an attempt to trap Daniel and cause him to be killed, the other presidents convinced King Darius to pass a law that no one could pray to any god for 30 days except to King Darius or they would be put into a den of lions. That law would rid them of Daniel because he was known for praying to his God. Daniel worshiped the Lord in defiance of the decree of King Darius. King Darius's faith in God was amazing when he said, "Thy God whom thou servest continually, he will deliver thee" (Daniel 6:16). Early the next morning when the king arrived at the lion's den,

> He cried with a lamentable voice unto Daniel: and the king spake and said to Daniel, O Daniel, servant of the living God, is thy God, whom thou servest continually, able to deliver thee from the lions?
>
> Then said Daniel unto the king, O king, live forever.
>
> My God hath sent his angel, and hath shut the lions' mouths, that they have not hurt me: forasmuch as before him innocency was found in me; and also before thee, O king, have I done no hurt. (Daniel 6: 20–22)

I would not have wanted to be the wife or child of the men that had accused Daniel, because "the king commanded, and they brought those men which had accused Daniel, and they cast them into the den of lions, them, their children, and their wives; and the lions had the mastery of them" (Daniel 6:24).

Another favorite story of protecting angels is the story of Elisha and the servant. The king of Syria found out that a prophet named Elisha was informing the king of Israel about his battle strategies. The king of Syria knew his strategy needed to change.

> Therefore sent he thither horses, and chariots, and a great host: and they came by night, and compassed the city about [where Elisha was].
>
> And when the servant of the man of God was risen early, and gone forth, behold, an host compassed the city both with horses and chariots. And his servant said unto him, Alas, my master! How shall we do?
>
> And he answered, Fear not: for they that be with us are more than they that be with them.
>
> And Elisha prayed, and said, Lord, I pray thee, open his eyes, that he may see. And the Lord opened the eyes of the young man; and he saw: and, behold, the mountain was full of horses and chariots of fire round about Elisha.
>
> And when they came down to him, Elisha prayed unto the Lord, and said, Smite this people, I pray thee, with blindness. And he smote them with blindness according to the word of Elisha. (2 Kings 6:14–18)

What a comforting message we are taught: angels that watch over us outnumber our adversaries. If our eyes could be opened, we would see these heavenly messengers as the servant of Elisha did.

Elder James E. Talmage said,

> Our eyes are so heavy, our ears so dull, that we see and hear only the things of earth. Could our vision be opened, we would see in this room at this very moment more worshippers than are occupying these seats; could our ears be unstopped we would hear more than our own feeble voices joining in the hymns of praise that we sing.
>
> When at times trouble comes upon us, and we feel almost given up to despair, and think we have been deserted by friends, let us think of the heavenly companions whom God has assigned to us; who, indeed, would reveal themselves to our eyes but for our lack of faith.[94]

Even if we are unable to see angels, we can have faith that they are there ready to assist us.

Jesus Christ reminded his Apostles that he could call down

legions of angels if he so desired. "Thinkest thou that I cannot now pray to my Father, and he shall presently give me more than twelve legions of angels? But how then shall the scriptures be fulfilled, that thus it must be?" (Matthew 26:53–54).

Early Church history is full of accounts of angels protecting the Saints. From the life of Heber C. Kimball, we get this account of angels protecting the saints in Zion's Camp:

> On Sunday, the 25th, we arrived at the edge of Illinois; we had no meeting but attended to washing and baking to prepare for our journey. On the 26th we resumed our march. At night we were alarmed by the continual threatening of our enemies. I would here remark that notwithstanding so many threats were thrown out against us, we did not fear, nor hesitate to proceed on our journey, for God was with us, and angels went before us, and we had no fear of either men or devils. This we knew because they (the angels) were seen.[95]

Fear is the opposite of faith. Knowing that there are angels ready to come to our assistance will help us overcome those feelings of doubt and distress. If we are willing to "look unto me [God] in every thought; [we will] doubt not, fear not" (D&C 6:36).

The angel Moroni was sent to protect the plates when Joseph and David Whitmer were leaving Harmony and headed to Fayette. David Whitmer, one of the Three Witnesses to the Book of Mormon, described what happened.

> A very pleasant, nice-looking old man suddenly appeared by the side of our wagon and saluted us with, "good morning, it is very warm," at the same time wiping his face or forehead with his hand. We returned the salutation, and, by a sign from Joseph, I invited him to ride if he was going our way. But he said very pleasantly, "No, I am going to Cumorah." This name was something new to me, I did not know what Cumorah meant. We all gazed at him and at each other, and as I looked around enquiringly of Joseph, the old man instantly disappeared. . .
>
> It was the messenger who had the plates, who had taken them from Joseph just prior to our starting from Harmony."[96]

Angels protect people, but from this story we learn they will even protect physical items that are precious to the Lord.

Elder Bruce C. Hafen shared this account and reminded us that angels are protecting us even when we cannot see them. He said, "The Prophet also 'saw Elder Brigham Young in a strange land, . . . in a desert place, upon a rock in the midst of about a dozen [hostile] men. He was preaching to them in their own tongue, and *the angel of God standing above his head,* with a drawn sword in his hand, protecting him, *but he did not see it.*'"

Continuing, Elder Hafen shared an experience Joseph Smith had when he saw the Savior Himself watching over the Apostles. "Recall when Joseph Smith 'saw the Twelve Apostles of the Lamb, . . . in foreign lands, standing together in a circle, much fatigued, with their clothes tattered and feet swollen, with their eyes cast downward, and *Jesus standing in their midst, and they did not behold Him.* The Savior looked upon them and wept.' "[97]

We see once again the emotions of the Lord. Was He weeping for the sacrifices of His special servants or for the wickedness of the people that rejected their message, or both? The Lord has not left them or us alone. President James E. Faust quotes David O McKay in relating this next story about the Martin Handcart Company. I have always loved the story because my husband's great-great-grandmother and his great-grandmother were members of the Martin Handcart Company. The early pioneers had many miraculous experiences. These angels assisted the Saints when they wanted to stop and just die.

> "A teacher, conducting a class, said it was unwise ever to attempt, even to permit them [the Martin Handcart Company], to come across the plains under such conditions."
>
> Then President McKay quoted an observer who was present in that class: "Some sharp criticism of the Church and its leaders was being indulged in for permitting any company of converts to venture across the plains with no more supplies or protection than a handcart caravan afforded.
>
> An old man in the corner . . . sat silent and listened as long as he could stand it, then he arose and said things that no person who heard him will ever forget. His face was white with emotion, yet he spoke calmly, deliberately, but with great earnestness and sincerity.
>
> In substance [he] said, "I ask you to stop this criticism. You are

> discussing a matter you know nothing about. Cold historic facts mean nothing here, for they give no proper interpretation of the questions involved. Mistake to send the Handcart Company out so late in the season? Yes. But I was in that company and my wife was in it and Sister Nellie Unthank whom you have cited was there, too. We suffered beyond anything you can imagine and many died of exposure and starvation, but did you ever hear a survivor of that company utter a word of criticism? . . .
>
> "I have pulled my handcart when I was so weak and weary from illness and lack of food that I could hardly put one foot ahead of the other. I have looked ahead and seen a patch of sand or a hill slope and I have said, I can go only that far and there I must give up, for I cannot pull the load through it."
>
> He continues: "I have gone on to that sand and when I reached it, the cart began pushing me. I have looked back many times to see who was pushing my cart, but my eyes saw no one. I knew then that the angels of God were there.
>
> "Was I sorry that I chose to come by handcart? No. Neither then nor any minute of my life since. *The price we paid to become acquainted with God was a privilege to pay, and I am thankful that I was privileged to come in the Martin Handcart Company.*"[98]

The Martin and Willie handcart companies lost many of their members as mentioned. Without the aid of angels, many more may have died. This account gives us a reason for our suffering; many of our trials are to sanctify us, and angels don't interfere with that process happening.

Elder John A. Widtsoe, a member of the Quorum of the Twelve Apostles, stated, "Undoubtedly angels often guard us from accidents and harm, from temptation and sin. They may properly be spoken of as guardian angels. Many people have borne and may bear testimony to the guidance and protection that they have received from sources beyond their natural vision. Without the help that we receive from the constant presence of the Holy Spirit, and from possible holy angels, the difficulties of life would be greatly multiplied."[99]

This quote brings up a question in regard to angels protecting us. Are there guardian angels? This is a common belief held by some that we have an assigned angel that is with us. Elder Widtsoe answers that question: "It is a very comforting thought, but at present without proof of its correctness. An angel may be a guardian angel though he come only as assigned to give us special help. In fact, the constant presence of the Holy Ghost would seem to make such a constant, angelic companionship unnecessary."[100]

The *Ensign* addressed this topic of guardian angels in March of 1988, in the segment called, "I Have a Question." Larry E. Dahl, associate professor of Church history and doctrine at Brigham Young University, answered the question, "Is there any truth to the idea that we have guardian angels who watch over and protect us?" He stated that several Church leaders have used the wording "guardian angels." He cited the following examples:

> In a blessing he pronounced upon Newel K. Whitney in October 1835, the Prophet Joseph Smith said, "Angels shall guard [his] house and shall guard the lives of his posterity." In June 1844, in a meeting in the Seventies Hall in Nauvoo, the Prophet related a dream he had had, in which, he said, "I thought I was riding out in my carriage, and my guardian angel was along with me." In July 1854, Elder Orson Hyde spoke of Moroni as "the guardian angel of America."[101]

Larry E. Dahl also shared a story from President David O. McKay. President McKay shared this story in a general conference in 1968.

> Following a series of meetings at the conference held in Glasgow, Scotland, was a most remarkable priesthood meeting. I remember, as if it were yesterday, the intensity of the inspiration of that occasion. Everybody felt the rich outpouring of the Spirit of the Lord. . . .
>
> During the progress of the meeting, an elder on his own initiative arose and said, "Brethren, there are angels in this room. . . ."
>
> President James L. McMurrin, president of the European Mission, arose and confirmed that statement by pointing to one brother sitting just in front of me and saying, "Yes, brethren, there are angels in this room, and one of them is the guardian angel of that young man sitting there," and he designated one who afterward became a patriarch. . . .
>
> Pointing to another elder, he said, "And one is the guardian angel of that young man there. . . ." Tears were rolling down the cheeks of both of these missionaries—not in sorrow or grief, but as an expression of the overflowing Spirit. Indeed, we were all weeping."[102]

However, Elder Bruce R. McConkie, of the Quorum of the Twelve Apostles, stated clearly that we do not have guardian angels. He said,

> But to suppose that either all men or all righteous men have heavenly beings acting as guardians for them runs counter to the basic revealed facts relative to the manner in which the Lord exercised his benevolent watchfulness over his mortal children. The fact that angels have intervened to preserve someone in a particular peril does not establish the fact that all people generally have guardian angels any more than the fact that angels have ministered to selected prophets would prove that angels have ministered to all men. Actually the preserving care of the Lord is exercised through the Light of Christ.[103]

The Savior was asked by His Apostles who is the greatest in the kingdom of heaven. The Lord called a little child to Him and taught His Apostles that unless they become as a little child they can't enter into the kingdom of heaven. He then taught them about not offending little children and then he makes an interesting statement. "Take heed that ye despise not one of these little ones; for I say unto you, *That in heaven their angels* do always behold the face of my Father which is in heaven" (Matthew 18:10; emphasis added).

We are left to wonder what the Lord meant when He said "their angels." What we do know is that angels can be sent to protect us.

Elder Dallin H. Oaks shared a story of being protected after giving us the promise that guardian angels would attend us in this mortal life.

> All over the world, faithful Latter-day Saints are protected from the powers of the evil one and his servants until they have finished their missions in mortality. For some the mortal mission is brief, as with some valiant young men who have lost their lives in missionary service. But for most of us the mortal journey is long, and we continue our course with the protection of guardian angels.
>
> During my life I have had many experiences of being guided in what I should do and in being protected from injury and also from evil. The Lord's protecting care has shielded me from the evil acts of others and has also protected me from surrendering to my own worst

> impulses. I enjoyed that protection one warm summer night on the streets of Chicago. I have never shared this experience in public. I do so now because it is a persuasive illustration of my subject."[104]

Elder Oaks and his wife, June, agreed to take a sister home after a church meeting. This sister lived in the Woodlawn area that was controlled by a local gang called the Blackstone Rangers. Elder Oaks walked the sister to her apartment lobby. He left the car keys in the car with his wife, June, just in case she needed to drive away from any potential danger. Before returning to the car he looked carefully down the street and saw three young men. He waited for them to walk past before returning to the car. One of the young men turned around and ran back before Elder Oaks could enter the car. He had something in is hand.

June saw the young man with the gun in his hand but she did not unlock the car door. Instead she sat in fear as she watched the events unfold. The gunman wanted Elder Oaks to hand over his wallet. There was no money in it but he did have a few coins in his pocket. He didn't even have a watch to give him. The young gunman was not interested in the coins and demanded the car keys. Elder Oaks told him no. He ordered him to unlock the car and give him the keys or he would be killed.

Elder Oaks refused even though he could see the gunman was becoming more agitated and he started jabbing the gun into his stomach. Elder Oaks became concerned that the gun would accidentally go off as he continued to jab at him. Once again the gunman repeated his demands for the money which Elder Oaks didn't have and the keys which he refused to give him.

June could not hear the conversation but could see the gun and began to wonder if she should unlock the door or honk the horn or drive away. Instead she waited and prayed.

A city bus arrived. A passenger got off and hurried away. The bus driver offered no help but drove away. This distracted the gunman long enough that the gun moved to Elder Oaks' left side and for the first time the thought came to him to grab the gun and wrestle it away from the gunman.

> Just as I was about to make my move, I had a unique experience. I did not see anything or hear anything, but I *knew* something. I knew what would happen if I grabbed that gun. We would struggle, and I would turn the gun into that young man's chest. It would fire, and he would die. I also understood that I must not have the blood of that young man on my conscience for the rest of my life.
>
> I relaxed, and as the bus pulled away I followed an impulse to put my right hand on his shoulder and give him a lecture. June and I had some teenage children at that time, and giving lectures came naturally.
>
> "Look here," I said. "This isn't right. What you're doing just isn't right. The next car might be a policeman, and you could get killed or sent to jail for this."
>
> With the gun back in my stomach, the young robber replied to my lecture by going through his demands for the third time. But this time his voice was subdued. When he offered the final threat to kill me, he didn't sound persuasive. When I refused again, he hesitated for a moment and then stuck the gun in his pocket and ran away. June unlocked the door, and we drove off, uttering a prayer of thanks. We had experienced the kind of miraculous protection illustrated in the Bible stories I had read as a boy.
>
> I have often pondered the significance of that event in relation to the responsibilities that came later in my life. Less than a year after that August night, I was chosen as president of Brigham Young University. Almost fourteen years after that experience, I received my present calling.
>
> I am grateful that the Lord gave me the vision and strength to refrain from trusting in the arm of flesh and to put my trust in the protecting care of our Heavenly Father. I am grateful for the Book of Mormon promise to us of the last days that "the righteous need not fear," for the Lord "will preserve the righteous by his power." (1 Ne. 22:17.) I am grateful for the protection promised to those who have kept their covenants and qualified for the blessings promised in sacred places.[105]

Remember, the term "guardian angel" is a term used when an angel protects us. That does not mean that we have an angel that is assigned to us. An angel may be sent one time to guard us from harm. The difficulty with the term guardian angel is how people view what a guardian angel is. Yes, angels can be sent to protect us. No, angels don't follow us around nor we are their sole responsibility.

When my children were young, a group of mothers in the neighborhood got together to form a carpool and take turns driving our children to the elementary school. We lived too close for bus service and we were too far away to feel comfortable letting our children walk along the busy roads. I had two children going to school at that time. David and Lisa were nineteen months apart and very competitive. When they were dropped off close to our house, they would race across the street to see who could get to the home first.

One day, I was talking to my good friend Gwen, when she expressed to me the horrifying experience she had days before when she dropped off my children. She drove a van and the kids had jumped out of the side door and David proceeded to race Lisa across the street. He ran in front of her van and started out into the street when Gwen saw in her side view mirror a car approaching the van. She said it happened so quickly that there was no way to stop the impending tragedy that she knew was about to occur. Instead, to her surprise, David was standing against her van and the car sped along not even aware of the close encounter. She wanted me to talk to my children about being more careful when they crossed the street. She said, "I don't know how that accident was avoided." She was extremely shaken by what could have happened.

I approached David and questioned him about the incident. He had been afraid to tell me what happened because he knew he would be in trouble for not looking both ways before crossing the street. Then he disclosed the rest of the story: He had started out without any thought of looking. He was only concerned about being the first one across the street, when he physically felt something push him back against the van. I was humbled to realize that David's life had been preserved or serious injury avoided because of divine intervention. His "guardian" angel was assuredly on duty—right by his side.

Elder Ronald A. Rasband, then in the presidency of the Seventy, shared a story of angels protecting a young girl from a tornado. He was sent on an assignment to Oklahoma City shortly after a massive tornado hit the area on May 20,2013. The storm covered 17 miles and was more than one mile wide. The tornado destroyed property and left devastation in the lives of the people of Oklahoma City.

Elder Rasband met with many of the families who had been effected by the storm. The Sorrels family was one of those families. Tori Sorrels, a fifth grader, shared an experience she had while at school.

> Tori and a handful of her friends huddled in a restroom for shelter as the tornado roared through the school. Listen as I read, in Tori's own words, the account of that day:
>
> "I heard something hit the roof. I thought it was just hailing. The sound got louder and louder. I said a prayer that Heavenly Father would protect us all and keep us safe. All of a sudden we heard a loud vacuum sound, and the roof disappeared right above our heads. There was lots of wind and debris flying around and hitting every part of my body. It was darker outside and it looked like the sky was black, but it wasn't—it was the inside of the tornado. I just closed my eyes, hoping and praying that it would be over soon.
>
> "All of a sudden it got quiet.
>
> "When I opened my eyes, I saw a stop sign right in front of my eyes! It was almost touching my nose."
>
> Tori, her mother, three of her siblings, and numerous friends who were also in the school with her miraculously survived that tornado; seven of their schoolmates did not.
>
> That weekend the priesthood brethren gave many blessings to members who had suffered in the storm. I was humbled to give Tori a blessing. As I laid my hands on her head, a favorite scripture came to mind: "I will go before your face. I will be on your right hand and on your left, and my Spirit shall be in your hearts, and mine angels round about you, to bear you up."
>
> I counseled Tori to remember the day when a servant of the Lord laid his hands on her head and pronounced that she had been protected by angels in the storm.[106]

My niece, Kristin, felt the protection of angels in a car accident she had while in high school. Kristin wrote,

> It was an amazing experience. My friends and I had the habit of attending the temple for the Tuesday morning session of baptisms. We had served that morning. I went that evening to drop Matt, my brother, off at a friend's home to study. I was a brand new 16-year-old driver, making a left hand turn at a busy intersection where there was no stoplight. The sun was going down in front of me which made my vision poor in that direction. I pulled out into the intersection so that I could better see the cars coming over the hill to my left, and in the

> time it took me to check to the right and look back to the left, and with a car in my rear and the one coming toward me motioning to go ahead I glanced back to my left and saw a large white Mercedes Benz coming at me. It hit me on my side of the car, smashing me into the center console of the car. The car was "totaled." I was very shaken up by the experience, but walked away from the accident without even a scratch or a bruise. I came home and said a prayer of thanks for my safety, and the safety of the woman who was driving the other car. As I finished the prayer, I felt the distinct impression that I had been protected by angels, some of whom were with me in the temple that morning. It was a very humbling experience I will never forget.

I have talked to many people that have felt a divine protection in time of need. As I was working on this book, I was talking with my son-in-law Jacob and he said, "I had a time as a young priesthood holder when I felt the help of angels." I asked him to share his experience with me. He said,

> As a deacon-aged boy, the ministering of angels was real. I was walking through a canyon with my friends and on the path were two young rattlesnakes. Both of them jumped at me and I was carried completely away from them. I remember thinking symbolically that Heavenly Father would not bless me and my loved ones with protection and safety by a small margin, but that He would bless us with safety far from danger. This was a witness to me that angels minister through Heavenly Father's direction and that we can feel that He truly is our Father. As an earthly father, I know that my desire is not to protect my children from the dangerous spiritual "rattlesnakes" by a small margin, but to get that as far away as possible.

I was pleased that the impression given Jacob was that Heavenly Father would keep us far away from danger. Jacob had not really shared this experience before, but when the discussion of angels came up, he was immediately drawn back to the feelings of that day when he sensed angels lifting him out of harm's way.

It is interesting that when you are looking for stories about angels that you begin to see angel stories everywhere. A tragic story was aired over the television, July 9, 2014, of a man that came to his sister-in-law's home looking for his estranged wife. He ordered the family to lay down face first and then shot each person. This included Cassidy

Stay, her parents, and four siblings. Cassidy had a fractured skull but she did not die. In a memorial service for her family, her grandfather talked about the bravery of this young fifteen-year-old. The family was an LDS family. Her grandfather, referring to Cassidy, told those at the memorial service:

> "Without her courage and quick thinking we might be mourning the deaths of 20—yes I said 20—including the deaths of myself and all of our children and grandchildren," he said.
>
> Lyon said soon after visiting Cassidy in the hospital, he learned how she managed to stay alive in a seemingly impossible situation.
>
> "While she was hospitalized Cassidy was generally lucid and made a miraculous recovery. Always talkative like her mother, Cassidy was able to tell us how she did it. She'd learned in Sunday school that God has the power to send his angels to protect his children in great need," said Lyon.
>
> "After she had been shot on Wednesday, she said it felt as though those angels were there with her, putting their hands over her mouth whispering to her to be quiet."[107]

Cassidy had been taught about angels and she recognized and credited angels for the divine assistance she received. Those angels helped protect her life as they kept her quiet and still until after the gunman left.

I have used the following two quotes previously in talking about the role of angels to help us repent. But have we ever thought to turn to angels to help protect us from sin? Elder Jeffrey R. Holland gave this counsel in a conference talk. He was addressing the addiction of pornography. He said, "Acknowledge that people bound by the chains of true addictions often need more help than self-help, and that may include you. Seek that help and welcome it. Talk to your bishop. Follow his counsel. Ask for a priesthood blessing. Use the Church's Family Services offerings or seek other suitable professional help. Pray without ceasing. *Ask for angels to help you.*"[108]

Elder Boyd K. Packer also advised us to turn to angels to help us resist Satan.

> Every soul confined in a prison of sin, guilt, or perversion has a key to the gate. The key is labeled 'repentance' If you know how to use

> this key, the adversary cannot hold you. The twin principles of repentance and forgiveness exceed in strength the awesome power of the tempter. If you are bound by a habit or an addiction that is unworthy, you must stop conduct that is harmful. *Angels will coach you*, and priesthood leaders will guide you through those difficult times.[109]

Angels can help protect us from sinning and strengthen us to resist temptation. They will also stand with us when we face opposition to the truth we have chosen to live. Elder Dallin H. Oaks taught us about the importance of standing up for our beliefs in a world that is crumbling because of moral indecency. He said,

> I turn now to the obligations of truth and tolerance in our personal relations with associates who use profanity in our presence, live with a partner out of wedlock, or do not observe the Sabbath day appropriately.
>
> Our obligation to tolerance means that none of these behaviors—or others we consider deviations from the truth—should ever cause us to react with hateful communications or unkind actions. But our obligation to truth has its own set of requirements and its own set of blessings. When we "speak every man truth with his neighbour" and when we "[speak] the truth in love" (Ephesians 4:15, 25), we are acting as servants of the Lord Jesus Christ, doing His work. Angels will stand with us, and He will send His Holy Spirit to guide us.[110]

The knowledge that we are not alone when facing opposition will give us the courage we need to make a stand even in the face of hatred and intolerance. It may also give us the tolerance we need to respond with respect and love.

Elder David A. Bednar gave the youth a special promise of protection from the adversary if they would do family history work. He said, "I promise you will be protected against the intensifying influence of the adversary. As you participate in and love this holy work, you will be safeguarded in your youth and *throughout your lives*."[111]

This safeguard against the adversary may very well be given by those for whom we are doing the saving ordinances. The following account was a physical protection given because of a sister's family history work.

This final story I will use as an example of angels protecting us comes from Connie Measom. I read Sister Measom's story and wanted to share it in this book. When I called to ask permission to use her story, I introduced myself and told her I had read the story. Before I could ask permission to use it she said, "Every word of that story is true. It happened just like I said." I had not called because I doubted the truthfulness, but it was a tender moment to hear this dear sister testify of the truthfulness of what she wrote. "It happened," she repeated, "just the way I wrote it."

> On June 23, 2012, a wildfire broke out in rural Sanpete County, Utah. The Wood Hollow fire, as it was called, will go down in history as one of Utah's most frightening wildfires. Fueled by erratic winds, it spread like napalm, destroying 108 structures, including 52 homes, and claiming the life of one. What follows is a personal account of Connie Measom, a resident of the area.
>
> My husband and I were enjoying the weekend camping with some of our children and grandchildren in Bryce National Park when we learned about the Wood Hollow fire.
>
> We knew the fire was approaching our neighborhood, and that our home and property—everything we had there—was in grave danger.
>
> Our first instinct was to end our camping trip and get to our house as fast as we could. But as we discussed the idea, we realized that since the area was being evacuated and the roads would be closed, there would be nothing we could do if we left. So we stayed where we were and worried and prayed.
>
> We drew comfort from our young grandchildren, who, with great faith and love, pled earnestly with their Heavenly Father, asking that "Grandma and Grandpa's house would not burn down."
>
> I prayed along with them in my heart. Our home in Indianola is very special to me, not only because it is a beautiful house in a beautiful setting, but because it was built entirely by my husband, a son-in-law and a grandson. A great deal of sweat and love went into that house.
>
> We called one of our daughters at her home, and asked her to drive to Indianola. Firefighters there allowed her to go into our house briefly to gather what she could. In the few minutes she had, she grabbed our computer, an armful of pictures and scrapbooks, and some of our important medications, wishing she could do more. As she was escorted out by the firefighter, she could see the fire

descending over the mountains—heading directly toward our home. Our prayers and worries grew more intense.

The next morning one of our neighbors called us and reported that the fire had passed through the area and that our home was still standing. He said we should expect some damage. With sadness in his voice, he told us that his home had been completely destroyed. They had lost everything.

Later that day, two of our daughters drove to Indianola, entering through a back road that had not been closed. As they drove toward our house, they saw the total devastation surrounding the area. The ground was black. All the trees and plants were gone. Many beautiful homes and vacation sites had burned to the ground. They approached our home with growing apprehension and worry.

When our daughter called us to report what they had seen, she said, "Mom, it's a miracle. I can't see one bit of damage to the home or garage. It looks like somebody put a circle around your yard and said to the fire, 'Don't burn in here.' "

Everything outside this circle was devastatingly burned. The fire came within a few feet of our trailers and other equipment, burning the surrounding area but leaving our equipment completely undamaged.

My daughter took pictures of our home and the area around it. When she showed them to her husband, who is an experienced fire-fighter, he was impressed with the skills of the firemen who were working in the area of our home. "They did a wonderful job of back-burning the property," he said. But we had been told that the fire-fighters had not been able to get into the area because of the height of the flames and the speed at which the fire was moving.

I was awestruck. I knew that this could not have happened by pure chance. And while I was enormously grateful, I also felt intense remorse and guilt because our home and property was spared, and so many of our good neighbors had lost everything. Overwhelmed by these powerful emotions, I retreated into the bedroom of our RV and prayed, "Lord, how did this happen?"

I will never forget what happened after I spoke those words. I distinctly heard a voice in my head say, "I will show you." Immediately I was filled with the Spirit so intensely that I thought I would burst. It filled my body from the tips of my toes to the top of my head. It was unlike anything I had ever felt before, and it was unmistakably from a divine source. As I knelt, paralyzed by what I was feeling, I saw what could only be called a vision. I was looking down at my home, watching the fire approach, and I saw a great army of men—perhaps hundreds of them—encircling our home. They appeared to be farmers, dressed in gray-white clothing. I did not recognize any of them. Each man stood with his back to the fire, his arms outstretched to touch the hands of the men next to him.

I saw the amazing scene for a very short time, but I received an understanding that all these men were my ancestors, those whose names I had labored for years to find; those who, through my steady efforts, were able to receive their temple ordinances. I understood that this was their gift to me—their way of saying thanks. I no longer felt guilty, because I knew that when a gift is given in love, it must be gratefully accepted.

The intensity of the Spirit departed, but I remained still, pondering the new awareness I had received. I understood why our house was still standing. I felt such appreciation for the love my ancestors had demonstrated for me. I rejoiced in my knowledge that these male progenitors had accepted the Gospel and received the Priesthood, something I had wondered about before.

I didn't tell anyone about this experience for a few days because it was so sacred and personal that I felt it might lessen it to share it. But then I came to know that just as this experience had enlightened me and strengthened my testimony, it could do the same for others.

With my children's encouragement, I have written this account so it will stand as a record and a testimony for my grandchildren, and for my posterity to come.

I bear solemn testimony of the reality of this event. I hope (or pray?) that throughout the remainder of my life I remember this experience and seek to obtain inspiration and personal revelation. I know that I will continue to seek out my ancestors and perform their temple work with a renewed determination and a surer understanding of the reality of the importance of this sacred work.

I told Sister Measom as she talked with me that I hoped she would not stop doing family history research. She reassured me that she labors every day in this work. Sister Measom's experience is a living testimony of John A. Widtsoe's statement that "those who give themselves with all their might and mind to this work [genealogical work] receive help from the other side. Whoever seeks to help those on the other side receive help in return in all the affairs of life."[112]

Who might those angels be that would care enough to weep

for us? Who would want to help protect us from sin and temptation? Who would step forward to try and protect us? We know who those individuals would be in this life. It would surely be our parents, family members, and close friends. President Joseph F. Smith stated his belief that it is our loved ones beyond the veil that would also perform that loving service for us.

> I believe we move and have our being in the presence of heavenly messengers and of heavenly beings. We are not separate from them. . . . We are closely related to our kindred, to our ancestors . . . who have preceded us into the spirit world. We cannot forget them; we do not cease to love them; we always hold them in our hearts, in memory, and thus we are associated and united to them by ties that we cannot break. . . . If this is the case with us in our finite condition, surrounded by our mortal weaknesses, . . . how much more certain it is . . . to believe that those who have been faithful, who have gone beyond . . . can see us better than we can see them; that they know us better than we know them. . . . We live in their presence, they see us, they are solicitous for our welfare, they love us now more than ever. For now they see the dangers that beset us; . . . their love for us and their desire for our wellbeing must be greater than that which we feel for ourselves.[113]

If righteous men and women are involved in the work of teaching and trying to bring the message of redemption to those in the spirit world who have rebelled, why would they distance themselves and leave their loved ones on earth to fend for themselves? I know as a mother I would do anything to bless my children and help them succeed no matter what side of the veil I was on.

President Harold B. Lee taught that angels would help us: "If our problems be too great for human intelligence or too much for human strength, we too, if we are faithful and appeal rightly unto the source of divine power, might have standing by us in our hour of peril or great need an angel of God."[114]

I am filled with peace when I place my faith in the Lord. If we keep our covenants, we are promised that we will be given the Lord's protection. We will have that protection and not be taken before our work on this earth is done.

President Joseph Fielding Smith said at the funeral services of

Elder Richard L. Evans, "And may I say for the consolation of those who mourn, and for the comfort and guidance of all of us, that no righteous man is ever taken before his time. In the case of the faithful Saints, they are simply transferred to other fields of labor. The Lord's work goes on in this life, in the world of spirits, and in the kingdoms of glory where men go after their resurrection."[115]

I have seen people live through horrible accidents when doctors have said they would die. I have also seen people who should not have died but who passed away. I had a student that was 16 years old. He was strong and healthy and played football for the high school. He was in class one day and a week later he was gone.

The *Deseret News* reported

> Timpview High School sophomore Parker McKay Allred was a big, healthy boy.
>
> At 16, the 6-foot-1, 200-pound Parker excelled at both football and water polo.
>
> But on Jan. 25, Parker began feeling ill with a fever. Within days he was just a "skeleton of his former self," according to a blog by his sister, Madison Allred.
>
> Early Saturday morning—just one week later—Parker died, reportedly from a combination of a staph infection and the flu, leaving an entire community in disbelief over his rapid and tragic decline.
>
> "That's the shocking thing, this great big 200-pound kid, great athlete, swimmer, football player, just a totally healthy kid a week ago," said one of his football coaches, Bryan Hopkins.[116]

The promise of President Joseph Fielding Smith that a righteous man will not die before his time is also given in the Doctrine and Covenants:

> And the elders of the church, two or more, shall be called, and shall pray for and lay their hands upon them in my name; and if they die they shall die unto me, and if they live they shall live unto me. (D&C 42:44)

The Lord makes the decision if we live or die. But if needed, angels will be sent to protect the righteous until the Lord calls them home.

The Lord will use His army of angels to protect those who are worthy. Heber C. Kimball pointed out the vast number of angels ready to come to our aid.

> The Lord has said that there are more for us than there can be against us. "Who are they," says one? Righteous men who have been upon the earth.
>
> But do you suppose that angels will pay friendly visits to those who do not live up to their privileges? Would you? . . . The God whom I serve . . . has millions of angels at His command. Do you suppose that there are any angels here today? I would not wonder if there were ten times more angels here than people. We do not see them, but they are here watching us and are anxious for our salvation. . ..
>
> The Lord has hosts of angels who are qualified to defend us, and they have information enough to march armies and to select leaders to lead them against the enemies of the Saints.[117]

My hope is that we walk with confidence through these troubled times knowing that we can receive assistance from angels. My testimony is echoed in the words of Heber C. Kimball: "This is the God that I believe in, and in him I put my trust. I know also that he will fight our battles from this time henceforth if we will only do right. He will turn our enemies aside and cause all things to work together for our good. Therefore, let us trust in him, and he will send his angels to watch over us, and he will preserve us as in the hollow of this hand."[118]

Chapter 11

Angels Warn

When we get behind the steering wheels of our cars, our eyes should be on alert for warning signs indicating sharp turns, uneven roads, and animal crossings. It is in our best interest to heed the warning signs. In a similar way, the Lord sends angels to warn and direct us through the difficulties of this life. There is an interesting account in the Old Testament of angels warning Lot, Abraham's nephew.

Three angels went to Lot in Sodom to warn him to leave the city before it was destroyed. (Genesis said there were two angels but Joseph Smith changed that number to three in the Joseph Smith Translation.)

> And the men said unto Lot, Hast thou here any besides? son in law, and thy sons, and thy daughters, and whatsoever thou hast in the city, bring them out of this place:
>
> For we will destroy this place, because the cry of them is waxen great before the face of the Lord; and the Lord hath sent us to destroy it. (Genesis 19:12–13)

The angels had to hasten Lot (see Genesis 19:15). Lot lingered and "the men laid hold upon his hand, and upon the hand of his wife, and upon the hand of his two daughters; the Lord being merciful unto him: and they brought him forth, and set him without the city" (Genesis 19:16).

The Lord never destroys a people without warning them about

what is going to happen. It is interesting that because of the mercy of the Lord, the angels made sure Lot was removed from the city. Lot's wife turned back and was destroyed and his daughters engaged in immoral acts. Even with the Lord's warning, Lot appeared to have lost everything he had.

Laman and Lemuel were also warned by an angel. However, these appearances seemed to have a very little impact on their hard hearts. Without the appearance of a heavenly messenger, Nephi and Sam surely would have been killed or injured badly by his murmuring brothers.

> And it came to pass as they smote us with a rod, behold, an angel of the Lord came and stood before them, and he spake unto them, saying: Why do ye smite your younger brother with a rod? Know ye not that the Lord hath chosen him to be a ruler over you, and this because of your iniquities? Behold ye shall go up to Jerusalem again, and the Lord will deliver Laban into your hands.
>
> And after the angel had spoken unto us, he departed.
>
> And after the angel had departed, Laman and Lemuel again began to murmur, saying: How is it possible that the Lord will deliver Laban into our hands? Behold, he is a mighty man, and he can command fifty, yea, even he can slay fifty; then why not us. (1 Nephi 3:29–31)?

This angel served several roles. The angel protected Nephi and Sam but warned Laman and Lemuel and then prophesied that Nephi would be a ruler over them.

The condition of our heart determines how receptive we are to heavenly visitors. For instance, Laman and Lemuel said of Nephi,

> Now, he says that the Lord has talked with him, and also that angels have ministered unto him. But behold, we know that he lies unto us; and he tells us these things, and he worketh many things by his cunning arts, that he may deceive our eyes, thinking, perhaps, that he may lead us away into some strange wilderness. . . . And after this manner did my brother Laman stir up their hearts to anger. (1 Nephi 16:38)

Those who are hard hearted have a difficult time believing in angels. Even though Laman and Lemuel had seen an angel themselves and the angel had told them Nephi would rule over them, they still denied that their father or brother Nephi could have seen angels and been instructed by them.

Alma the Younger was delivered a warning as well as instructions from an angel because of the prayers of his father and the righteous Saints. The angel not only warned but threatened Alma with spiritual destruction that lay ahead of him if he did not repent. The angel said,

> Nevertheless he cried again, saying: Alma, arise and stand forth, for why persecutest thou the church of God? For the Lord hath said: This is my church, and I will establish it; and nothing shall overthrow it, save it is the transgression of my people.
>
> And again, the angel said: Behold, the Lord hath heard the prayers of his people, and also the prayers of his servant, Alma, who is thy father; for he has prayed with much faith concerning thee that thou mightest be brought to the knowledge of the truth; therefore, for this purpose have I come to convince thee of the power and authority of God, that the prayers of his servants might be answered according to their faith.
>
> And now behold, can ye dispute the power of God? For behold, doth not my voice shake the earth? And can ye not also behold me before you? And I am sent from God. . . .
>
> And now I say unto thee, Alma, go thy way, and seek to destroy the church no more, that their prayers may be answered, and this even if thou wilt of thyself be cast off. (Mosiah 27:13–16)

Alma was warned that he was no longer to destroy the Church. He was warned that he would be "cast off" if he continued. The angel makes it clear that he was "sent from God" to deliver the warning to Alma. This warning produced great results. Alma spent the rest of his life proclaiming the gospel and calling others to repent as well as his companions, the sons of Mosiah.

Joseph was warned to take the baby Jesus to Egypt. "The angel of the Lord appeareth to Joseph in a dream, saying, Arise, and take the young child and his mother, and flee into Egypt, and be thou there until I bring thee word: for Herod will seek the young child to destroy him" (Matthew 2:13). This angel not only warned of impending danger but also protected Jesus from harm.

Joseph Smith appeared to Brigham Young and left a warning for the Church. This account is told by Wilford Woodruff. "One morning, while we were at Winter Quarters, Brother Brigham Young said to me and the brethren that he had had a visitation the night previous from Joseph Smith. I asked him what he said to him. He replied that Joseph had told him to tell the people to labor to obtain the Spirit of God; that they needed that to sustain them and to give them power to go through their work in the earth."[119] This is an important warning for us today. We too need to obtain the Spirit of Lord. The Holy Ghost is the most important gift we have been given in this life to give us power to do the work the Lord requires of us.

Elder Parley P. Pratt told of an account of an angel waking him up and telling him he had to leave.

> At noon I had turned my horse loose from the carriage to feed on the grass in the midst of a broad, level plain. No habitation was near; stillness and repose reigned around me; I sank down overpowered with a deep sleep, and might have lain in a state of oblivion till the shades of night had gathered about me, so completely was I exhausted for want of sleep and rest; but I had only slept a few moments till the horse had grazed sufficiently, when a voice, more loud and shrill than I have ever before heard, fell on my ear, and thrilled through every part of my system; it said: 'Parley, it is time to be up and on your journey.' In the twinkling of an eye I was perfectly aroused; I sprang to my feet so suddenly that I could not at first recollect where I was, or what was before me to perform. I related the circumstance afterwards to Brother Joseph Smith, and he bore testimony that it was the angel of the Lord who went before the camp, who found me overpowered with sleep, and thus awoke me.[120]

We may get an impression that we should do something and not know the reason why that impression came. Parley P. Pratt was not given the reason why he had to leave. President Harold B. Lee has a similar situation where he is told not to do something but he did not have any idea what would have happened if he had not obeyed.

> I have a believing heart that started with a simple testimony that came when I was a child—I think maybe I was around ten or eleven years of age. I was with my father out on a farm away from our home, trying to spend the day busying myself until my father was

> ready to go home. Over the fence from our place were some tumble-down sheds that would attract a curious boy, and I was adventurous. I started to climb through the fence, and I heard a voice as clearly as you are hearing mine, calling me by name and saying, "Don't go over there!" I turned to look at my father to see if he were talking to me, but he was way up at the other end of the field. There was no person in sight. I realized then, as a child, that there were persons beyond my sight, for I had definitely heard a voice. Since then, when I hear or read stories of the Prophet Joseph Smith, I too have known what it means to hear a voice, because I've had the experience.[121]

Listening to a voice and not knowing why a request is being made may be a test of our willingness to obey. I know I have failed that test many times. I am grateful that the Lord gives us many chances to prove ourselves trustworthy. These warnings were also a test of faith. Neither Elder Parley P. Pratt nor President Lee knew why they were to obey. They also didn't know the consequences of being disobedient. We may never know the reason why we are prompted by the Lord, the Holy Ghost, or angels but following the warnings are essential.

Joseph Smith was warned by the angel Moroni that his very name would be known for good and evil. That warning became prophetic.

> He called me by name, and said unto me that he was a messenger sent from the presence of God to me, and that his name was Moroni; that God had a work for me to do; and that my name should be had for good and evil among all nations, kindreds, and tongues, or that it should be both good and evil spoken of among all people. (Joseph Smith—History 1:33)

There are not many lukewarm people when it comes to Joseph Smith. There are those who say horrible things about him. And there are those that sing with great vigor, "Praise to the Man that communed with Jehovah. . . . Hail to the Prophet ascended to heaven! Traitors and tyrants now fight him in vain. Mingling with Gods, he can plan for his brethren; Death cannot conquer the hero again."[122] The Lord reiterated Moroni's warning and told Joseph, "The ends of the earth shall inquire after thy name, and fools shall have thee in derision, and hell shall rage against thee; While the pure in heart, and the wise, and the noble, and the virtuous, shall seek counsel, and authority, and blessing constantly from under thy hand" (D&C 122:1–2). That warning/prophecy is still seen in full effect nearly two hundred years later.

In a previous chapter, I explained that patriarchs in the Church of Jesus Christ of Latter-day Saints could be described as angels. They are messengers for the Lord and they speak by the power of the Holy Ghost. Patriarchs pronounce God's prophecies of possibilities for an individual's life. They likewise pronounce many warnings. If you want to see your patriarchal blessing in a new light, divide a sheet of paper into three columns. In the first column list those statements in your blessing that talk about who you are and your potential. In the next column, list those items that describe what the Lord prophesies about you and what you can achieve if you are faithful. In the third column, list the warnings and counsel the Lord gives you. I have done this and it helped me analyze my blessing and allowed me to easily see the warnings the Lord gave me. Then it is up to us to avoid those pitfalls.

I received a warning one day and unfortunately, I totally disregarded it. The consequences could have been devastating. I am embarrassed to admit that I am such a stubborn person. My family and I had moved into a newly built home. I had an appointment with my son to fix my car. I was making soup for dinner that night and wanted to get it started before I left. I had the gas burner on high and was worried I would leave it on high too long, making the soup burn or boil over on the stove. I checked the heat and turned the gas burner as low as it would go before leaving. I jumped in the car and I heard a voice say, "check the stove." I thought to myself, *I checked the stove.* I started up the hill and once again the voice said, "Check the stove." I thought, *You know there is a sickness when people think they have left the iron on and have to check it multiple times. I know I turned down the heat and I am not going back.* Once again the voice said, "Check the stove." I thought to myself, *No, I am not crazy, I am not going to go back because I remember turning the stove down.*

I got to the auto body shop at my son's work, and he was doing a rush job on another car and didn't have time to work on mine for at least 45 minutes to an hour. I decided instead of waiting for him I would borrow his car and leave mine with him and have him drop off mine later in the day.

When I arrived home and opened the door to the kitchen, I was shocked at how strong the gas smell was in the house. I choked as I ran in and checked the stove. The flame was out and gas was pouring into the house. I quickly turned off the stove and opened windows and doors until the gas dissipated. I felt so disobedient. I had been told clearly three times to check the stove. We have a gas fireplace in the family room next to and adjoining the kitchen with a pilot light that is always burning. I was mortified to think that my house could have blown up that day. I felt so blessed that I went straight home. Any warning given is only beneficial if we heed the warning.

Harold B. Lee said, "If our problems be too great for human intelligence or too much for human strength, we too, if we are faithful and appeal rightly unto the source of divine power, might have standing by us in our hour of peril or great need an angel of God."[123]

Chapter 12

Angels of Comfort

Mercifully, angels are sent to give comfort.

"So amid the conflict, whether great or small, Do not be discouraged; God is over all. Count your many blessings; angels will attend, Help and comfort give you to your journey's end."[124]

As shown above, in the hymn "Count Your Blessings," we are told that angels will help and give us comfort. What a beautiful promise for being thankful and recognizing where our blessings come from. Showing gratitude does bring comfort even if angels are not sent to our aid.

Once again, we see in the scriptures examples of angels comforting those in need. Nephi and Lehi were put into prison after they had successfully taught and converted eight thousand Lamanites. The Lord sent angels to protect and comfort them. Aminadab saw angels conversing with Nephi and Lehi in prison, "and they were filled with that joy which is unspeakable and full of glory" (Helaman 5:44).

Not long before Christ came to the Americas to minister, we have another righteous prophet named Nephi who had the blessing of having angels minister to him daily as he worked among a wicked people. "And it came to pass that they were angry with him [Nephi], even because he had greater power than they, for it were not possible that they could disbelieve his words, for so great was his faith on the Lord Jesus Christ that *angels did minister unto him daily*" (3 Nephi 7:18; emphasis added).

After the Savior's first visit with the righteous Nephites, the people gathered to wait for Jesus Christ to come again. The twelve disciples that the Savior had called the day before were teaching and baptizing the multitude that had gathered. The disciples "were encircled about as if it were by fire; . . .and angels did come down out of heaven and did minister unto them" (3 Nephi 19:14).

When the Savior visited the Nephites, it was a glorious time for the people and there were many instances of angels coming to minister to the Nephites. The most touching account of angels visiting during the Savior's ministry was when the people "saw the heavens open, and they saw angels descending out of heaven as it were in the midst of fire; and they came down and encircled those little ones about, and they were encircled about with fire; and the angels did minister unto them" (3 Nephi 17:24). As a mother and grandmother, it would bring so much joy and comfort to see my little ones encircled about with angels. The Savior's visit and the ministering of angels would influence these people's lives for the next two hundred years.

The scriptures teach us when the Savior returns during the second coming that once again angels will accompany Him. "When the Son of man shall come in his glory, and all the holy angels with him, then shall he sit upon the throne of his glory" (Matthew 25:31). Angels work in tandem with the Lord.

Mormon and Moroni had the privilege of having angels that were translated beings minister and bring comfort to them. Mormon and Moroni would be the last two righteous people to witness the destruction of the Nephite nation. "But behold, my father and I have seen them, and they have ministered unto us" (Mormon 8:11). The three angels that visited in this verse were the three Nephite disciples who were translated when Jesus came to the Nephites.

Each of these accounts bears testimony of the Lord sending heavenly angels to inspire comfort and peace. I think the most moving example in all scripture of an angel being sent to comfort is in Luke when an angel is sent to comfort the Savior in the Garden of Gethsemane:

> Saying, Father, if thou be willing, remove this cup from me: nevertheless not my will, but thine, be done.
>
> And there appeared an angel unto him from heaven, strengthening him.
>
> And being in an agony he prayed more earnestly: and his sweat was as it were great drops of blood falling down to the ground. (Luke 22:42–44)

I love Carl Bloch's painting (*Gethsemane*) showing the Savior in the arms of the angel.[125] The expressions on their faces emanate the agony of the Savior and the love of that heavenly being.

Although according to LDS doctrine angels do not have wings, this picture illustrates the comfort this angel gave to the Savior as He suffered in the Garden of Gethsemane. Christ's suffering was so great that even He, the greatest of all, needed the comfort of a heavenly being.

Who might have been given that glorious privilege of comforting the Savior in Gethsemane? Of all the angels at the command of God, who would be the one to be at the side of our suffering Lord?

Elder Bruce R. McConkie speculated on who that angel might have been.

> And if we might indulge in speculation, we would suggest that the angel who came into this second Eden was the same person who dwelt in the first Eden. At least Adam, who is Michael, the archangel—the head of the whole heavenly hierarchy of angelic ministrants—seems the logical one to give aid and comfort to his Lord on such a solemn occasion. Adam fell, and Christ redeemed men from the fall; theirs was a joint enterprise, both parts of which were essential for the salvation of the Father's children.[126]

What a touching encounter this event would have been to see Adam, who brought about the Fall, comforting our Lord, who overcame all the effects of that Fall. If the Savior needed angels in His sojourn in life, how much more do we need angels?

Elder Jeffrey R. Holland expresses the fact that the Savior needed comfort from angels during his mortal ministry as well as in Gethsemane. "Even the Son of God, a God Himself, had need for heavenly comfort during His sojourn in mortality. And so such ministrations will be to the righteous until the end of time."[127]

Moroni, who needed comfort himself from the three Nephite translated angels, would be the angel to comfort Mary Whitmer. Moroni appeared to Mary Whitmer to comfort her when she was feeling overburdened with the extra work that was placed upon her as she cared for Joseph and Emma during the translation of the Book of Mormon. This account was given by her grandson, John C. Whitmer in 1878:

> I have heard my grandmother (Mary Musselman Whitmer) say on several occasions that she was shown the plates of the Book of

Mormon by a holy angel, whom she always called Brother Nephi. (She undoubtedly refers to Moroni, the angel who had the plates in charge.)

It was at the time, she said, when the translation was going on at the house of the elder Peter Whitmer, her husband. Joseph Smith with his wife and Oliver Cowdery, whom David Whitmer a short time previous had brought up from Harmony, Pennsylvania, were all boarding with the Whitmers, and my grandmother in having so many extra persons to care for, besides her own large household, was often overloaded with work to such an extent that she felt it to be quite a burden.

One evening, when (after having done her usual day's work in the house) she went to the barn to milk the cows, she met a stranger carrying something on his back that looked like a knapsack. At first she was a little afraid of him, but when he spoke to her in a kind, friendly tone and began to explain to her the nature of the work which was going on in her house, she was filled with inexpressible joy and satisfaction. He then untied his knapsack and showed her a bundle of plates, which in size and appearance corresponded with the description subsequently given by the witnesses to the Book of Mormon. This strange person turned the leaves of the book of plates over, leaf after leaf, and also showed her the engravings upon them; after which he told her to be patient and faithful in bearing her burden a little longer, promising that if she would do so, she should be blessed; and her reward would be sure, if she proved faithful to the end. The personage then suddenly vanished with the plates, and where he went, she could not tell.

From that moment my grandmother was enabled to perform her household duties with comparative ease, and she felt no more inclination to murmur because her lot was hard. I knew my grandmother to be a good, noble and truthful woman, and I have not the least doubt of her statement in regard to seeing the plates being strictly true. She was a strong believer in the Book of Mormon until the day of her death."[128]

The angel Moroni's comfort gave Mary Whitmer a reason to endure. When we understand the reason for the burden we are carrying, it makes the load more bearable. Mary Whitmer was able to bear testimony of the great work that was being done in her home. Hyrum L. Andrus, a well-known author of numerous books on Church history, shared this account:

> A young woman of about twenty years of age was working for the Whitmer family as a hired girl when Joseph and Oliver were completing the translation of the Book of Mormon at the Whitmer home. She later related that when they came down from the room in which they were working, "they looked so exceedingly white and strange that she inquired of Mrs. Whitmer the cause of their unusual appearance." Finally, Mrs. Whitmer "told her what the men were doing in the room above and that the power of God was so great in the room that they could hardly endure it. At times angels were in the room in their glory which nearly consumed them."[129]

This young woman was able to actually see a physical change in Joseph Smith and Oliver Cowdery as they worked in the presence of angels.

My mother, Mary Ellen Larsen, was given comfort after the death of her younger brother Beaman. This is her account:

> I really mourned Beaman's passing as did all the family. Never had the death of father, mother, or anyone affected me as Beaman's death affected me. I could not get over it. I had such a pain each time I thought of him. It was a physical, hurting, heavy pain in my breast. It weighed so heavily on my mind and heart.
>
> His suffering had been so intense, we had prayed and fasted that he could go. I read Doctrine and Covenants 42:48–51 many times. "And again, it shall come to pass that he that hath faith in me to be healed, and is not appointed unto death, shall be healed. He who hath faith to see shall see. He who hath faith to hear shall hear. The lame who hath faith to leap shall leap." I knew it was a blessing that he could go on but I hurt and would find myself crying and so sad. It is a hard feeling to explain unless one has experienced the heaviness and sorrow that lingers on and on.
>
> I can't tell if I was awake or asleep when this experience occurred, but Beaman stood at the foot of my bed one night.
>
> I could only see his face and it was surrounded by a cloud-like substance. Beaman's face radiated. I had not seen Beaman look that happy for years. His skin was the most beautiful color. His face was full, his eyes shined. He was so close and vivid, even the space between his teeth showed. He had the biggest, happy smile I have ever seen. His visit didn't last long and I cannot explain too much more about his appearance. All I can say is, he looked in the prime of

> his life. He looked beautiful and had a radiance I can never explain nor can I ever forget.
>
> I had the sweetest, most comforting feeling I have ever experienced. A peace came to me that I can never forget or deny. The hurt was gone. Beaman is happy. The sad memories were taken away. I can hardly recall the sad memories, just that sweet, healthy, happy, smiling face.
>
> I am so grateful for this experience. I doubt I will ever have such an experience again but I can never forget or deny this special one. I am so thankful I was blessed with the privilege of seeing Beaman again.

Sister Almena Thorpe Wells, wife of Bishop John Wells, formerly of the Presiding Bishopric, had a similar experience to that of my mother's after the death of her son in a tragic train accident that took his life.

> A son of Bishop Wells was killed in Emigration Canyon on a railroad track. His boy was run over by a freight train. Sister Wells was inconsolable. She mourned during the three days prior to the funeral, received no comfort at the funeral, and was in a rather serious state of mind. One day soon after the funeral services, while she was lying on her bed relaxed, still mourning, she claims that her son appeared to her and said, Mother, do not mourn. Do not cry. I am all right. He told her that she did not understand how the accident happened. He explained that he had given a signal to the engineer to move on and then made the usual effort to catch the railings on the freight train, but as he attempted to do so his foot caught in a root and he failed to catch the hand rail and his body fell under the train. It was clearly an accident. He said that as soon as he realized that he was in another environment he tried to see his father but he could not reach him. *His father was so busy* with the duties in the office that he could not respond to his call; therefore, he had come to his mother and he said to her, you tell Father that all is well with me. I want you to not mourn anymore.[130]

This account makes us wonder if the busyness of our lives deprives us of sacred experiences. Is our life too busy with the duties of the day? We could also have the problem that we constantly have noise. Do we set aside time to ponder and feel? I have the problem that as soon as I stop to ponder, I think of a dozen other tasks that need my attention. Elder Marvin J. Ashton of the Quorum of the Twelve Apostles said, "By pondering, we give the Spirit an opportunity to impress and direct."[131] It also gives angels an opportunity to communicate with us.

The *Ensign* carried a story about a young girl named Sherrie Grigg. The doctors found that she had a rare tumor that grows in the spinal cord called astrocytoma. They had to do surgery on her to remove this tumor. The surgery was very difficult, but she had the comfort of angels from the other side. She told her Father, Clayne, about those that were there to help her.

> Following the surgery, Clayne and Debbie spent the day praying fervently and taking turns keeping vigil at Sherrie's bedside. As he watched his red-haired daughter sleep in a curtained cubicle that night, Clayne worried that she might die, as Dr. Walker had warned. But Sherrie awoke the next morning and immediately began speaking. A feeling of reverence engulfed the cubicle. For a moment, Clayne was puzzled by Sherrie's words.
>
> "Daddy, Aunt Cheryl is here" she told her father. "And another lady I don't know is with her." Clayne and an attending nurse, the only ones at Sherrie's bedside, glanced at each other. Sherrie continued.
>
> "Grandpa Norman [Sherrie's deceased great-grandfather] and Grandma Brown [Sherrie's deceased great-great-grandmother] are here. And Daddy, who is that standing beside you?"
>
> "I don't know, honey," Clayne replied. "Who does he look like?"
>
> "He looks like you, only taller." Sherrie paused, then continued. "He says he's your brother, Jimmy."
>
> Clayne was three when Jimmy, ten years his senior, died of cystic fibrosis. "I doubt that during Sherrie's life Jimmy's name had ever been mentioned," Clayne says. "She had never even seen a picture of him."
>
> Clayne, feeling that Sherrie's death was imminent, hurried from the intensive care unit to awaken Debbie, who was sleeping in the hospital's parent room. "There are visitors," he told his wife. "I can't see them, and I doubt that you can see them. But I can feel them."
>
> For nearly an hour, Sherrie looked about the cubicle and described her visitors, all deceased family members. Exhausted, she then fell asleep.
>
> "Daddy, all of the children here in the intensive care unit have

> angels helping them," Sherrie later told her father. Other visits and sacred experiences, before and after subsequent surgeries and during painful tests and procedures, followed.
>
> "People from the other side helped," Sherrie recalls tearfully. "When I was really in pain, they would come and help me calm down. They told me that I would be okay and that I would make it through."[132]

Sherrie was not left alone. Angels were sent to comfort her and help her feel calm. It is interesting that her father could feel them but not see them. He may not have needed the same kind of comfort that Sherrie did. Elder Holland said, "In times of special need, He sent angels, divine messengers, to bless His children, reassure them that heaven was always very close and that His help was always very near."[133] In Sherrie's account, it was her departed family members that brought her comfort.

Elder Robert D. Hales was in need of that special comfort from angels when he was in the hospital. He expressed how angels had comforted him after extensive health problems. "I also learned that I would not be left alone to meet these trials and tribulations but that guardian angels would attend me. There were some that were near angels in the form of doctors, nurses, and most of all my sweet companion, Mary. And on occasion, when the Lord so desired, I was to be comforted with visitations of heavenly hosts that brought comfort and eternal reassurances in my time of need."[134]

President Harold B. Lee shared his testimony of "guardian" or comforting angels. He told the story of a little girl that had the blessing of having her departed mother comfort her.

> I heard this little flaxen-haired girl sing "I Am a Child of God." "Lead me, guide me, walk beside me, help me find the way." The first time I heard it, this little girl sang it to her mother's accompaniment. Now [her] mother is gone. But the mother came to this little girl in such a vivid dream that she said the next morning, "Oh, Mother was with us. We saw her in the family room, and I said, Oh, Mother, you're not dead." And she said, "No my dear, I am not dead, I am very much alive. You won't be able to see me all the time, but I won't be far away from you, my dear." And with that childish assurance, the little girl is now growing to womanhood. Lead me, guide me,

> walk beside me, help find the way. Guardian angels? Don't you mistake it. It isn't your father and mother who will be far away from you, children; *it will be you who keep them far away. . . .*
>
> The Prophet Joseph Smith taught: "The spirits of the just are exalted to a greater and more glorious work hence they are blessed in their departure to the world of spirits." Now listen to this: "Enveloped in flaming fire, they are not far from us, and know and understand our thoughts, feelings, and motions, and are often pained therewith." . . .there will come times when you will say, "My, he seemed to be so close to me. I seem to have felt his nearness." And it will be real. *It will be something you can't deny.*
>
> Let this [funeral] not be a time of abject sorrow, but realize that your father might return to you as your holy guardian, limited in his scope but there when you need him the most. How do you know but that he may be very close and very near on occasions when such a messenger would be very valuable?[135]

In President Lee's statement, he said that it would be our action that would keep angels away. For those who are in need and have faith to believe, angels can bring comfort in time of need while those that deny the existence of angels cut themselves off from this tender mercy. Mormon stated it like this: "it is by faith that angels appear and minister unto men; wherefore, if these things have ceased wo be unto the children of men, for it is because of unbelief, and all is vain" (Moroni 7:37).

President Harold B. Lee shared a story of receiving a priesthood blessing from an angel. This blessing served to protect President Lee's life but also to give him the comfort and ability to get to the proper medical help.

> I was suffering from an ulcer condition that was becoming worse and worse. We had been touring a mission; my wife, Joan, and I were impressed the next morning that we should get home as quickly as possible. . . .
>
> On the way across the country, we were sitting in the forward section of the airplane. Some of our Church members were in the next section. As we approached a certain point en route, someone laid his hand upon my head. I looked up; I could see no one. That happened again before we arrived home, again with the same experience. Who it was, by what means or what medium, I may never

> know, except I knew that I was receiving a blessing that I came a few hours later to know I needed most desperately.
>
> As soon as we arrived home, my wife very anxiously called the doctor. . . . He called me to come to the telephone, and he asked me how I was; and I said, "Well, I am very tired. I think I will be all right." But shortly thereafter, there came massive hemorrhages which, had they occurred while we were in flight, I wouldn't be here today talking about it.[136]

This blessing kept President Lee comfortable and safe until he was in a situation to get the proper medical care. At the time of the blessing, he did not realize that his life was in jeopardy.

This next account has angels providing comfort in a time of tragedy. Our good friends were able to recognize the help of angels in their life. Alan and Christina have been given more challenges and trials to overcome than most people I know. These trials seem to sanctify and refine them. I never see them lose faith or hope. Christina shared some special experiences they had after their son-in-law was killed in a car accident. Christina wrote the following:

January 30, 2005

> When Catherine called us on the side of the freeway after the car accident to tell us Kimball had been badly injured; we jumped in the car and began to drive from Provo to Bountiful where the accident happened. We took turns praying out loud the entire way. I began to pray for angels to minister to him, to help him. A friend was on the freeway after the accident so we knew the freeway was congested because of the emergency vehicles. Yet we somehow got there very quickly and called the police to find out to which hospital the family was taken. Just as we found out, we got off at the correct exit without delay and were directed to the hospital. We arrived as they brought in Scott and Taylor from the ambulance and could comfort them until their mother and the younger two children arrived 10 minutes later. Alan went to the University of Utah hospital where Kimball was life-flighted. He found out Kimball had died in flight and called me so I could give Catherine the news. I was able to do that before the police came in to tell her.
>
> We found out later as we talked about the events of that night

with others that angels were involved in several ways in answer to our prayers:

- The family was traveling in the far left lane of the freeway when the accident happened. Catherine somehow guided the car over the 2–3 lanes of freeway to stop it at the side of the road without hurting anyone else though it was dark, smoke was in the car from the air bags firing, and she was trying to use her left leg to somehow brake the car though that side was smashed in against Kimball. In other words, she was not alone; someone helped her do it safely.
- We arrived in record time to a congested area and got there to comfort the children and Catherine. A way was opened up for us.
- Alan and I examined the demolished car in the days that followed and were astonished to see the wreckage and the glass strewn everywhere. We both felt it was truly miraculous that anyone walked away from the accident. Yet all of the family escaped with minor injuries except for Kimball. I came away feeling that they had had angels covering their eyes to protect them from the glass.
- From a blessing given to Alan's mother, we learned that her husband, Roger, who had died many years earlier in a plane crash, had been with Catherine's family along with other angels to protect the rest of the family.
- Catherine's bishop lives close to her and often looked out his front door toward her house wondering how to help her. He has seen angels as sentinels around her house protecting her family. Our home teacher has seen angels as sentinels during this time around our home protecting us as well.
- We had written several pages of tender mercies we had recognized over the months preceding the accident, during, and after the accident. It was an important list. However, I accidently left it at the church where the funeral was held. I was heartsick. No one knew where it was located. That evening or the next day, I found that notebook in the upstairs middle bedroom and again no one knew how it got there.
- Over the years when things got difficult for Catherine, I have asked for help from her husband and my mother who died 3 days after Kimball died. Catherine has felt the presence of her husband many times, especially in times of stress and doubt.

I am amazed at the divine help given this wonderful couple in such a tragic time of their lives. I am even more amazed that they were able to recognize this help and see the Lord's hand in their lives and the comfort He gave them.

The next story is a very personal account to me. My son left home at eighteen to go to college. He started to experiment with everything he had ever wondered about. I had so many dreams and expectations for this young man and it was destroying me to watch him die spiritually and there was nothing I could do to stop it. It was obvious that he was using drugs. His eyes were dull and glazed. One day he rode home on his motorcycle. As he was leaving, I stood talking to him for a short time in the front yard. He had straddled his motorcycle. I looked at him and cried out in my mind, "Please, Heavenly Father, I don't want to love this child anymore. It hurts so badly. He is killing me. Please take away my love for him." Instead of removing the love from my heart, my heart was enlarged, feeling even greater love than before. I cried out as I walked into the house in tears, "No Lord, not more love, no love!"

I realized, however, I couldn't stop loving him no matter what he did. No matter how badly he hurt me, I would always love him. I felt love in every fiber of my being for this wayward son. I had a greater understanding come to me at this time of the love the Lord has for each of us. This love is called charity, the true love of God. I understood how the Lord could love a rebellious disobedient child. I loved my son as intensely as I had ever loved him, maybe even more. I knew God's love was perfect. I knew He loved me more perfectly than I would ever be able to understand but I had a little glance into the power of that love.

On another occasion, I was once again in the temple pouring out my heart to the Lord for the return of this dear son. I had just raised my head and was sitting pondering when a young man approached me. There were many missionaries in the temple that day so I was not drawn to pay attention to any one in particular. The young man came over to me and knelt down on one knee and put his hand on top of my hands. I was so stunned that a complete stranger had approached me in such an intimate way that I was in total shock wondering what he was doing. He said very softly to me, "Sister, the Lord has heard thy prayers." He paused and looked into my eyes then he stood up went over to the other missionaries and they left the room. I sat frozen trying to process what had just happened to me. Who was he? Why did he say that to me? What does he know of my heartache? Why would he walk up to a total stranger and say that? Then my mind said again the words he had spoken, "Sister, the Lord has heard thy prayers." All of a sudden a rush of emotion filled my breast with warmth and love. I felt the Lord's love for me ripple through my being and tears swelled up in my eyes. I just sat there basking in the love and warmth knowing that God was so aware of what I had been pleading for, for so many years. Then it hit me, why didn't I ask him why he would come and talk to me? What prompted a nineteen-year-old to walk up to a perfect stranger and say those words? How was he assigned to be an agent or angel for the Lord to deliver that message? I determined that I would quickly dress and wait outside the temple and try and find him before he returned to the MTC. I waited for about thirty minutes. Missionaries left the temple but I never saw him. I thank the Lord for the sweet words of love and encouragement and comfort sent by a missionary angel.

The Lord has not left us comfortless. "I will not leave you comfortless: I will come to you" (John 14:18). This is the Lord's promise that he would send the Holy Ghost to give us comfort. The Holy Ghost is our greatest comforter, but in special circumstances He will also send angels. My grandmother, Leona Snow Albrechtsen, who has passed away, received her patriarchal blessing on June 6, 1894. She was promised that she would be comforted by angels. "The Lord hath thee in special keeping. He hath delegated angels fresh from the courts of heaven to minister unto thee. Thou shalt be comforted, thy joy shall be great here and hereafter." I don't think this promise is unique just to her. The Lord will also delegate angels to comfort us.

Chapter 13

Destroying Angels

Does God actually appoint angels to destroy? One of the unique and often overlooked missions of angels is that of destruction.

Our Heavenly Father is a God of delegation. In order to bring about all His righteous purposes, there need to be servants empowered to kill and otherwise destroy or to administer His judgments. Godly destruction—verses satanic destruction—is calculated to avenge unrighteousness, but with the long-term goal of endeavoring to redeem, if only his children will accept that redemption.

One analogy that might illustrate the role of an "avenging angel" is when the children of God are disobedient and absolutely refuse to be taught in this life and try to destroy the prophets and messengers sent to save them, there is only one choice left, put them in time-out. Much like parents who put their children that are out of control in time-out, Heavenly Father removes the disobedient, bent on their own destruction and the destruction of everything and everyone around them, and puts them in time-out (which is the spirit prison). When defiance, hostility, and refusal to comply are ongoing, it requires serious intervention.

The Lord finally had to intervene in the day of Noah. President Joseph F. Smith was given a vision of the spirit world, which is now referred to as Doctrine and Covenants section 138. Prior to receiving this vision, he had been pondering several verses in 1 Peter that read, "Which also he [Christ] went and preached unto the spirits in prison; Which sometime were disobedient, when once the longsuffering of God waited in the days of Noah, while the ark was a preparing, wherein few, that is, eight souls were saved by water" (D&C 138:8–9).

Joseph F. Smith saw those disobedient souls that were destroyed in the flood. But Christ opened up the channels for them to be taught the gospel. This is a good example of the Lord trying to rescue and redeem those that no longer would listen or repent in this life.

God's destruction is for the purpose of redeeming man. Satan's purpose in destroying is to make us his slaves, chained in the addictions of our sins, which in turn destroys our happiness. He "sought also the misery of all mankind" (2 Nephi 2:18).

The Lord states, "This is my work and my glory—to bring to pass the immortality and eternal life of man" (Moses 1:39). This verse teaches us that the Lord has a divine plan. The Lord's work is to redeem mankind. Whenever He destroys anything or anyone, it is calculated to bless and redeem those who are involved, including future generations.

The scriptures teach of angels sent to destroy different groups of people for different reasons. For instance, destroying angels killed all the first born in Egypt.

Doctrine and Covenants 89, the section known as the Word of Wisdom, contains a promise for us about destroying angels. "And I, the Lord, give unto them a promise, that the destroying angel shall pass by them, as the children of Israel, and not slay them" (D&C 89:21).

This verse teaches us that one of the promises given if we follow the Word of Wisdom involves angels who will pass by us in times of destruction. Keeping the Word of Wisdom is like putting lamb's blood on our doorposts; the destroying angel will also pass by. Many times good and righteous individuals die during natural disasters. We may assume that they have finished their work upon the earth or they would be preserved.

It is instructive to learn in the Old Testament how the Lord used destroying angels. First, these angels were used to smite sinful Israelites, and second, to fight their battles. The Second book of

Samuel records an instance when destroying angels fulfilled the Lord's command:

> So the Lord sent a pestilence upon Israel from the morning even to the time appointed: and there died of the people from Dan even to Beer-sheba seventy thousand men.
>
> And when the angel stretched out his hand upon Jerusalem to destroy it, the Lord repented him of the evil, and said to the angel that destroyed the people, It is enough: stay now thine hand. (2 Samuel 24:15–16)

The pestilence was sent upon the people because David numbered the Israelites. David had the choice of three punishments. He could choose seven months of famine, three months as a fugitive, or three days of pestilence.

The Lord also used destroying angels to fight the Israelite's battles. For instance, destroying angels fought the Assyrian army using pestilence in 2 Kings. This time, destroying angels were used to protect those living in Jerusalem from the Assyrian army.

Jerusalem was surrounded by the Assyrian army that had captured the Northern ten tribes. This mighty army was invincible. The Lord sent angels to fight a battle that the Jews could not have possibly won on their own, yet it was won without shooting an arrow.

> For I will defend this city, to save it, for mine own sake, and for my servant David's sake.
>
> And it came to pass that night, that *the angel* of the Lord went out, and smote in the camp of the Assyrians an hundred fourscore and five thousand: and when they arose early in the morning, behold, they were all dead corpses.
>
> So Sennacherib king of Assyria departed, and went and returned, and dwelt at Nineveh. (2 Kings 19:34–36; emphasis added)

Sennacherib, king of Assyria, found that he could not fight a war without an army. Israel was truly protected by angels without shooting a single arrow.

The book of Revelation teaches of destroying angels ready to cleanse the earth in preparation for the Second Coming. Joseph Smith asks the Lord to explain some passages in the book of Revelation.

> Q. What are we to understand by the four angels, spoken of in the 7th chapter and 1st verse of Revelation?
>
> A. We are to understand that they are four angels sent forth from God, to whom is given power over the four parts of the earth, to save life and to destroy; these are they who have the everlasting gospel to commit to every nation, kindred, tongue, and people; having power to shut up the heavens, to seal up unto life, or to cast down to the regions of darkness. (D&C 77:8)

John the Revelator saw those destroying angels ready to descend on the earth and destroy it. However, it was not yet time to release the destroying angels.

> And after these things I saw four angels standing on the four corners of the earth, holding the four winds of the earth, that the wind should not blow on the earth, nor on the sea, nor on any tree.
>
> And I saw another angel ascending from the east, having the seal of the living God: and he cried with a loud voice to the four angels, to whom it was given to hurt the earth and the sea,
>
> Saying, Hurt not the earth, neither the sea, nor the trees, till we have sealed the servants of our God in their foreheads. (Revelation 7:1–3)

In other words, don't allow the angels to reap down upon the earth until the Lord has prepared His people. The Lord will warn and in some cases plead with the inhabitants to repent before they are destroyed. Many are not prepared because they do not heed the warning. I like the imagery that Isaiah gives of the Lord continually reaching out to save us even when we are disobedient.

> Therefore the Lord shall have no joy in their young men, neither shall have mercy on their fatherless and widows; for every one of them is a hypocrite and an evildoer, and every mouth speaketh folly. For all this his anger is not turned away, but his hand is stretched out still. (2 Nephi 19:17)

The Doctrine and Covenants reminds us of the chilling events that will yet occur before the Savior returns. After reading this verse, we do not have to wonder how the angels feel about the time in which we are living.

> For all flesh is corrupted before me; and the powers of darkness

prevail upon the earth, among the children of men, in the presence of all the hosts of heaven—

> Which causeth silence to reign, and all eternity is pained, and the angels are waiting the great command to reap down the earth, to gather the tares that they may be burned; and, behold, the enemy is combined. (D&C 38:11–12)

The angels are ready to enact destructions as soon as the Lord gives them permission to move forward. President Wilford Woodruff, in a discourse given on June 24, 1894, stated that those destroying angels are no longer waiting to be released but are starting the destruction promised in the scriptures. Notice that the date of this revelation is 1894. Can you recognize that those destroying angels have been released?

> God has held the angels of destruction for many years, lest they should reap down the wheat with the tares. But I want to tell you now, that those angels have left the portals of heaven, and they stand over this people and this nation now, and are hovering over the earth waiting to pour out the judgments. *And from this very day* they shall be poured out. Calamities and troubles are increasing in the earth, and there is a meaning to these things. Remember this, and reflect upon these matters. If you do your duty, and I do my duty, we'll have protection, and shall pass through the afflictions in peace and in safety. Read the scriptures and the revelations. They will tell you about all these things. Great changes are at our doors. The next twenty years will see mighty changes among the nations of the earth. You will live to see these things, whether I do or not. I have felt oppressed with the weight of these matters, and I felt I must speak of them here. It's by the power of the gospel that we shall escape.[127]

It is frightening to watch this development of destruction occurring around us. When we watch the nightly news, a common theme is natural devastation as well as man-induced destruction. As we watch destruction increase in these the last days, we will need the promise of protection given to us by the Lord. The Lord will continue to warn us by different methods to repent and be prepared, and angels will also continue to call out to us to be prepared for what lies ahead.

> How oft have I called upon you by the mouth of my servants, and

> by the *ministering of angels*, and by mine own voice, and by the voice of thunderings, and by the voice of lightnings, and by the voice of tempests, and by the voice of earthquakes, and great hailstorms, and by the voice of famines and pestilences of every kind, . . . and would have saved you with an everlasting salvation, but ye would not! (D&C 43:25; emphasis added)

In this next verse we see angels delivering the Lord's warning of the destruction that they know is coming perhaps by their hand. "The angels are crying unto the Lord day and night, who are ready and waiting to be sent forth to reap down the fields;" (D&C 86:5).

Brigham Young taught that the scriptures spoke of elements that "shall melt with fervent heat" (2 Peter 3:12). Then he said, "The Lord Almighty will send forth his angels, who are well instructed in chemistry, and they will separate the elements and make new combinations thereof, and the whole heavens will be a sheet of fire."[138]

Angels can easily carry out the Lord's instructions. Brigham Young further states that they know their chemistry and how to control the elements. The scriptures confirm the great power that angels possess. Here are a few examples:

- When Christ was resurrected, the scriptures tell us that Mary Magdalene and the other Mary came to the sepulcher (Matthew 28:1).

> And, behold, there was a great earthquake: for the angel of the Lord descended from heaven, and came and rolled back the stone from the door, and sat upon it.
>
> His countenance was like lightning, and his raiment white as snow:
>
> And for fear of him the keepers did shake, and became as dead men. (Matthew 28:2–4)

- The angel that appeared to Alma caused the earth to shake.

> The angel of the Lord appeared unto them; and he descended as it were in a cloud; and he spake as it were with a voice of thunder, which caused the earth to shake upon which they stood. (Mosiah 27:11)

- Herod killed James the brother of John and imprisoned Peter in hopes of killing him also. But the Lord destroyed Herod.

> And immediately the angel of the Lord smote him, because he gave not God the glory: and he was eaten of worms, and gave up the ghost. (Acts 12:23)

One of the responsibilities of angels is to carry out destruction upon man or upon the earth as these verses demonstrate. Angels can destroy in a variety of ways by moving rocks, shaking the earth, killing with disease, and hurting the earth and the seas. Angels have the power to accomplish the acts the Lord commands.

President N. Eldon Tanner shared an account in general conference from the life of Wilford Woodruff, when a destroying angel protected him while he was serving in the Aaronic Priesthood.

> We should all realize that great works of righteousness can be and are performed by the Aaronic Priesthood. President Wilford Woodruff relates an experience that he had. He said:
>
> "I was strongly impressed three times to go up and warn Father Hakeman [an early apostate]. At last I did so, according to the commandment of God to me. The third time I met with him, his house seemed to be full of evil spirits, and I was troubled in spirit at the manifestation. When I finished my warning, I left him. He followed me from his house with the intention of killing me. I have no doubt about his intention, for it was shown to me in vision. When he came to where I was, he fell dead at my feet, as if he had been struck with a thunderbolt from heaven. I was then a Priest, but God defended me and preserved my life. I speak of this because it is a principle that has been manifest in the Church of God in this generation as well as in others. *I had the administration of angels* while holding the office of a Priest. I had visions and revelations."[139]

President Wilford Woodruff does not specifically state if it was an angel that destroyed Father Hakman. But Father Hakman was destroyed and President Woodruff didn't kill him. These angels of destruction can help us fight our physical battles if we are living worthily.

President Heber C. Kimball promised us the help of angels in fighting our battles if we live righteously:

> Let us be one; let us try and live so that all will be as one man, or one drop of water, and thus partake of each other's principles and attributes, and the attributes of God, that angels may be our associates by night and by day. If this people will take this course, and live their religion in all things, I can prophesy in the name of Israel's God that you will never have to fire a gun, for *the Lord will send his angels to do the work of destruction among the wicked.* The Almighty will lead the wicked as a man leads a horse, at pleasure. Brethren, why don't you live your religion, magnify your callings and honour God in all things you do and say?[140]

The promise of angels fighting for our protection has comforted many mothers and fathers as they have sent their children out on full-time missions and into battle in defense of their country. However, this is a promise to each of us whether we are serving a full-time mission or simply needing the Lord's help with personal problems: "But I say unto you: Mine angels shall go up before you, and also my presence" (D&C 103:20).

Chapter 14

Not All Angels Are Good

I love to hear the word "angel." To me, it brings feelings of sweetness, goodness, and hope. It is instructive, however, in our discussion of angels to understand that Lucifer is he who (with all his followers—or angels) represents all that is contrary to the life, light, and love of Jesus Christ. Brigham Young stated that the "difference between God and the Devil is that God creates and organizes, while the whole study of the Devil is to destroy. . . . I call evil inverted good."[141] In other words, the devil takes the teachings of the Savior and turns them inside out, making Satan's teachings and purposes counterfeit and destructive.

Satan and his followers, who are sometimes referred to as angels, are driven in exactly the opposite direction of the Savior and His angels. The Savior's name means "one who redeems or rescues." On the other hand Satan's name means "to destroy—totally," and his mission is to dismantle all of Christ's teachings and to accuse us. (see Revelation 12:10)[142]

It is important to have a healthy understanding of the adversary and the dark, destructive powers he possesses. It is more useful to cling to the Savior with all our heart, might, mind, and strength. Rather than a bottomless pit of endless despair, concentrate on the endless beauty of the eternities ahead. Keeping that thought will always bless us to choose good instead of evil. However, we cannot be left unaware of the devil's role.

If we were to study the references in the standard works about angels, not all of the references would refer to angels from the Lord. Satan and his minions unfortunately play a prominent role in most of our lives. Satan is relentless in his opposition to all things good. That opposition is important as we grow and use our agency. Lehi described,

> For it must needs be, that there is an opposition in all things. If not so, . . . righteousness could not be brought to pass, neither wickedness, neither holiness nor misery, neither good nor bad. (2 Nephi 2:11)

When Mormon is teaching his son, Moroni, about Satan and Satan's purposes, he explained to him how to judge righteously between things that destroy and those that redeem. "All things which are good cometh of God; and that which is evil cometh of the devil" (Moroni 7:12). Mormon gave his son this key: Satan and his angels persuade men not to do good and not to believe in Christ our redeemer.

> For behold, the Spirit of Christ is given to every man, that he may know good from evil; wherefore, I show unto you the way to judge; for everything which inviteth to do good, and to persuade to believe in Christ, is sent forth by the power and gift of Christ; wherefore ye may know with a perfect knowledge it is of God.
>
> But whatsoever thing persuadeth men to do evil, and believe not in Christ, and deny him, and serve not God, then ye may know with a perfect knowledge it is of the devil; for after this manner doth the devil work, for he persuadeth no man to do good, no, not one; neither do his angels; neither do they who subject themselves unto him. (Moroni 7:16–17)

Mormon enables us to know if something comes from God or is just a thought you had or from someone more sinister. The key is if it persuades us to do good and believe in Christ, it is from the Lord.

In a book about angels, why would we discuss Satan? President Harold B. Lee taught this about Satan and his angels:

> Lucifer succeeded in persuading one-third of all the spirits to rebel. He and they were cast out upon the earth without mortal bodies and he became Satan. Some have seen his satanic majesty in his spiritual

> form, in bodily shape like a man. Some have seen individuals who have been possessed of evil spirits. Others there are who have felt the awful influence of his hellish suggestions. All of you have known individuals who because of their own sins are in his power and subject to his will. Make no mistake about his reality as a personality although he is not possessed of a physical body. Since the beginning of time he with his hosts, who are likewise beings in spiritual form, have waged relentless war to destroy the free agency of man and to lead captive as many as would not hearken unto the voice of the Lord (Moses 4:4).[143]

Unfortunately, Satan has influenced all of us. Even though he is unseen, he is still very real. President Lee's comment about knowing people who, because of their sins, are in Satan's power and are subject to his will, reminds me of an experience that our son had on his mission where he was introduced to the reality of Satan's power. He served in Concepcion, Chile. This email was sent to us on January 3, 2005. A man brought his friend, named Victor, to church. They left in the middle of the meeting because Victor was not feeling well. After fast and testimony meeting some members came to the missionaries and told them that someone needed a blessing. In the email my son wrote,

> What I saw I will never forget. Victor looked like he was having a seizure and his friend was trying to hold him down in a chair. I realized there was something more because he was raising his torso like he wanted to escape. He was possessed by something. We grabbed both of his arms. Some of the members came and helped us give him a blessing. My companion gave Victor the blessing and cast out the devil. After the blessing Victor just fainted and we brought in some chairs and laid him down. He was into some pretty dark things and wanted to change his life. We went to his house and burned all of his satanic stuff. His parents were amazed that Victor allowed us to burn those things. Afterwards we knelt down with his parents and sanctified the house. Victor's father was in tears when we finished. Victor had never seen his father cry. I learned something yesterday that the devil is definitely real. Before I didn't even believe in those kind of things but now I know.

I bring up this email not because it is unique. Many missionaries have this kind of experience. I bring it up because my son didn't believe that Satan had that ability or power to do what he did. In writing a book about angels, we need to know that Satan is real. But we do not have to fear him. The Prophet Joseph Smith left us with this great realization, "All beings who have bodies have power over those who have not. The devil has not power over us *only as we permit him*. The moment we revolt at anything which comes from God, the devil takes power."[144]

Another instance of a person allowing Satan into their life is demonstrated by a story a good friend shared with me. Our friend's work brought him to Utah from another state. After being in the ward several months, he was called to be the bishop of his new ward. The stake president, in issuing the call, said that among this new bishop's responsibilities there was a man in his ward that was causing considerable trouble preaching false doctrine. John (named changed) was affecting many members of the ward—and in the region—with flattering words and anti-Christ sentiments. The new bishop discovered that this man was always outwardly cordial and courteous, but very cunning.

The previous bishop of the ward had had John teaching the youth in Sunday school, hoping it might help him feel the Spirit. John was cautious not to preach anti-Mormon, or anti-Christ ideas to the youth, but was rather "philosophical" in his approach. John sowed seeds of doubt and twisted half-truths.

John was having marital and family problems and the new bishop met with him often. In his last interview with him, John couldn't contain himself, and the devilish, satanic nature came out in the open. John realized he had unzipped the sheep's clothing and exposed the wolf inside. John went home, told his wife he was leaving her for another woman, and was out of the house. He gleefully took a position with a local college where he could teach "philosophy" and use it as a platform to teach anti-Mormon, anti-Christ ideas. To this day, John takes great pleasure in teaching LDS students—especially those preparing for missions—and challenging their testimony. He became most adept at making his students feel spiritually dead. Even the young men in his ward suffered from his worldly ideas. The new bishop spent many hours counseling with these young men trying to help them see the errors in the doctrines they had been taught. John has been excommunicated from the Church, but he still does everything in his power to halt the kingdom of God.

Lucy Mack Smith, Joseph Smith's mother, stated that Moroni showed Joseph the difference between good and evil. This lesson made a lasting impact on Joseph's life. Lucy said, "The angel showed him by contrast, the difference between good and evil, and likewise the consequences of both obedience and disobedience to the commandments of God, in such a striking manner, that the impression was always vivid in his memory until the very end of his days; and in giving relation of this circumstance, not long prior to his death, he remarked, that ever afterwards he was willing to keep the commandments of God."[145]

Satan's joy comes from our captivity. *All* sin is extremely addictive. "He leadeth them by the neck with a flaxen cord, until he bindeth them with his strong cords forever" (2 Nephi 26:22). We cannot afford to entertain corruption in any degree. How many innocent people have been caught in Satan's traps thinking that just this once won't hurt, only to find they are unable to break free of his shackles?

Spencer W. Kimball explained how Satan captivates his victims. He said,

> It is true that the great principle of repentance is always available, but for the wicked and rebellious there is serious reservation to this statement. For instance, sin is intensely habit-forming and sometimes moves men to the tragic point of no return. . . . As the transgressor moves more deeply and the will to change is weakened, it becomes increasingly near hopeless, and he skids down and down until either he does not want to climb back or he has lost the power to do so.[146]

The longer we sin, the more difficult it is to repent of that sin. A characteristic like gossiping does not get easier to overcome. I have met individuals that have become so addicted to gossiping that it becomes the sum total of their conversation. The extent of their conversation is what so and so did, wore, or said.

The war for the souls of men, which began in the premortal world, is still being waged with heavenly hosts and satanic legions fighting for our allegiance. We decide whom we listen to. We decide which side of the battle we are willing to fight for. When we respond to the Spirit, we would do well to remember, "Behold, this is pleasing unto your Lord, and the angels rejoice over you" (D&C 88:2).

Even the Savior himself faced the master destroyer. Before the Savior started His mortal ministry, He fasted and prayed. It was at this time that the devil appeared to tempt Him. It was after resisting the devil's ploys that the scriptures say angels appeared unto Him.

> Then saith Jesus unto him, Get thee hence, Satan: for it is written, Thou shalt worship the Lord thy God, and him only shalt thou serve.
>
> Then the devil leaveth him, and, behold, angels came and ministered unto him." (Matthew 4:10–11)

We are not alone in the fight against evil. The Lord has promised to arm us with His help, the Holy Ghost's help, and His angels to support us. How then can we fail?

I think it would frighten us to realize the efforts that Satan and his host extend trying to stop the work of the Lord from going forth and to stop us from performing that work even to go so far as to keep us from going to the temple where we gain the power to resist his fiery darts. Temples are a place where the veil is so very thin, where many people have encounters with those that have gone on before. It is the source of great spiritual power.

President Boyd K. Packer said, "Temples are the very center of the spiritual strength of the Church. We should expect that the adversary will try to interfere with us as a church and with us individually as we seek to participate in this sacred and inspired work. Temple work brings so much resistance because it is the source of so much spiritual power to the Latter-day Saints, and to the entire Church."[147]

I had an encounter with one of those satanic spirits one day. I will call my friend Jill for this story. It was a Sunday and Jill had not come to Church. I was worried that she might be sick or not feeling well, so when I got home from Church I gave her a call but no one answered. I jumped in the car and drove to her home. When I got there the lights were all out. I started knocking on the door and calling out to her. The door finally opened a crack but she didn't speak. I walked into the room and reached out for Jill. As I touched her, she jumped as if an electric current had gone from me through her. She shut the door making the room completely dark. I told her I was going to turn on the light. She begged me not to do so, but I insisted the light be turned on. She rolled up on the floor in a fetal position. We talked for over an hour and I told her that I wanted to call my husband and another priesthood holder and have them cast the evil spirit out of her home. It took a long time to convince her but she finally agreed. My husband arrived with the ward high priest group leader. Jill's body was stiff, rigid, and shaking. When they placed their hands on her head and commanded the evil spirit to depart, I saw her body go completely limp. Her breathing became relaxed and there was a calm peaceful feeling that replaced the agony and despair of a few minutes earlier.

I never again want to feel the utter despair, emptiness, and darkness that I felt that evening. Satan has the ability to leave us feeling hopeless and worthless. He desires to have us experience feelings of despair and worthlessness. These feelings are his tools to discourage us and invite him into our lives. You will notice that when you are filled with the Spirit those feelings are not generally present. Another way we invite Satan into our lives is through anger and contention.

A friend of mine told me a story one day that has never left me and that caused me to seriously reflect on this principle of contention:

Contention

> For me to share this story, I have to give you sufficient background that you can understand my frame of mind, because I am not very proud of what I did. However, the lesson learned was powerful and will never to be forgotten. After twelve years of marriage and five children, the youngest was one month old, my husband confessed one night that he had been having an affair. Over the next month or so I began to learn from others (and he confirmed the truth) that this 'one short' affair he confessed to that night, was only the tip of the iceberg. As the old saying goes 'the wife is the last to know,' I found out he had been cheating on me for years with several different women and everyone in our small farming community in Idaho

knew it, including my own parents who had seen him once with another woman. And no one ever told me. I was very naïve and even though I felt something was wrong about our marriage I had never honestly thought adultery was the problem. You see I had prayed very hard before I married this man, and I believed that I had had confirmation from the Lord that he was the right man. We had a temple marriage and surely he wouldn't be breaking his temple covenants, as well as his marriage vows.

After a brief period of shock and another of sadness, I got into the healing step of *anger*—big time. I was angry at everybody. My husband was at the top of the list, but I was angry with friends who had known and instead of coming to me, they cut me off. I was angry at my parents who knew and siblings who had been informed and even investigated claims that my husband was cheating on me. I was angry at myself for being so blind and so believing. And worst of all I was angry with God. I believed he had let me down. I asked the Lord during our dating period if marrying him was right and I believed I had had a positive answer. And over the course of our marriage I had been trying to do all the right things, living the gospel and trying to raise our children in the right way.

In this state of mind I was struggling to hold the marriage together. My husband was promising to make changes and to never do it again. With five young children and never having worked outside the home, I felt staying with my husband was best, if not my only option. He went through Church disciplinary councils and was disfellowshipped. I was trying to be noble and do the right thing by forgiving him, but the anger was really challenging to deal with.

We took a family trip to Salt Lake City to stay in a time-share my husband had bought into about a year before. He had visited it many times for 'business,' but this was the first time the family had been invited to go along. Of course, I now understood it was 'monkey business.' The time-share was about a block away from Temple Square and I made the decision to leave him with the five children and go do a temple session. My attitude was not so much that I needed the quiet and peace of the temple, but, that I had a reason to leave him with the children and do something he couldn't do.

I entered the temple that day with a 'just try and show me something' attitude. (Which is the part of the story I regret). It was, of course, in the Salt Lake Temple so it was a live session. I found myself sitting in the session having my own pity party and paying very little attention to what was going on. In fact I would have to say I was ignoring what was going on around me completely. The angry feelings and the thoughts that I was so justified to have them, permeated my whole soul.

There is a part in the temple ceremony where Satan is commanded to leave. I don't remember hearing those words at all that day, as I sat in my own little shell, but I will never forget the feeling that I had. This is the only way I know how to explain it. There were two people sitting in that chair that day and I felt one of them get up out of my body and walk out the door. I was stunned. I suddenly paid attention to the ceremony going on around me and realized that Satan had been commanded "in the name of Jesus Christ to depart" and he did. He departed out of me. To this day when I remember this it makes me cry to realize that I had taken an evil spirit into the temple with me that day. And my testimony of evil spirits and entertaining them inside ourselves became an amazing reality. I vowed on that day that I would never do that again. Every time I prepare to go to the temple, I look deep inside myself to be sure that I am humble and that there is only one "striving to be good" spirit inside me that day.

I share this story only because of the thing I learned. I have no doubt about the truthfulness of our gospel. And the truthfulness of our temple work.

We need to stop and reflect on our lives before we enter the temple. The Lord has given us the great blessing and responsibility to act as saviors to those who have passed on without having their temple work done. We go to the temple to serve others. Those individuals may have been waiting for hundreds of years for someone do to their work, and we need to give them our best as we perform those sacred ordinances. The scriptures state,

> He that hath the spirit of contention is not of me, but is of the devil, who is the father of contention, and he stirreth up the hearts of men to contend with anger, one with another.
>
> Behold, this is not my doctrine, to stir up the hearts of men with anger, one against another; but this is my doctrine, that such things should be done away. (3 Nephi 11:29–30)

We need to resolve any unkind feelings we may feel toward others before we enter the temple. This principle does not just relate to the temple however. If we want to have the Spirit in our personal, everyday lives, we need to forgive and dismiss anger and contention from our lives.

> Therefore, if ye shall come unto me, or shall desire to come unto me, and rememberest that thy brother hath aught against thee—
>
> Go thy way unto thy brother, and first be reconciled to thy brother, and then come unto me with full purpose of heart, and I will receive you. (3 Nephi 12:23–24)

It is interesting to note in this verse that your neighbor has offended you. It didn't say if you have offended someone, go ask for their forgiveness, even though that thought is implied. Forgiving those that have hurt us is a very difficult struggle that we all deal with. That puts a heavy burden on our shoulders to be clean when we desire to enter into the Lord's presence, whether in personal prayer, in the Lord's house, or in His eternal kingdom.

Brigham Young gives us a warning that we should be aware of. When we have wonderful spiritual experiences, Satan will be there to provide opposition.

> God never bestows upon His people, or upon an individual, superior blessings without a severe trail to prove them, to prove that individual or that people, to see whether they will keep their covenants with Him, and keep in remembrance what he has shown them. Then the greater the vision the greater the display of the power of the enemy. So when individuals are blessed with visions, revelations, and great manifestations, look out, then the Devil is nigh you, and you will be tempted in proportion to the visons, revelations or manifestation you have received.[148]

The philosophy in our home has been to avoid anything that has to do with Satan. We seldom, if ever, speak of him. We respect that fact that he is real and powerful and we choose not to invite him in even in conversation. Joseph Smith said, "As well might the devil seek to dethrone Jehovah, as overthrow an innocent soul that resists everything which is evil."[149] In our attempt to keep his influence out of our lives and home, we choose not to speak of him, read about him, or see entertainment that depicts him.

Respect Satan but do not have anything to do with him. He will use your sympathies or any inroad given him to destroy you. It is so important that we live worthily so we keep ourselves armed against the devil's potential destructive power.

President Boyd K. Packer gave this warning;

> I must tell you so that you cannot possibly misunderstand: 'There are many spirits which are false spirits.' There can be counterfeit revelations, promptings from the devil, temptations! As long as you live, in one way or another the adversary will try to lead you astray. . ..
>
> If ever you receive a prompting to do something that makes you feel uneasy, something you know in your mind to be wrong and contrary to the principles of righteousness, do not respond to it![150]

In summary, we need to recognize that evil is real and is constantly there. We are so blessed to have the gift of the Holy Ghost and the Light of Christ that will warn us, if we are righteous, when we are approaching those gray areas. I love President James E. Faust's statement, "We need not become paralyzed with fear of Satan's power. He can have no power over us unless we permit it. He is really a coward, and if we stand firm, he will retreat."[151] And we can know that the Lord will send angels to our aid.

Chapter 15

Lay Claim to Your Promises

One of the reasons I chose to write this book was to remind us of one of the heavenly aids in our lives, even the ministering of angels.

This is not to say that those outside of the Church do not receive the blessing of angels appearing to them. That would be a false idea. What it does mean, to members of the Church *who are living righteously*, is that we can have unimpeded access to all heavenly ministrations through Aaronic Priesthood and Melchizedek Priesthood keys.

The Doctrine and Covenants tells us that blessings are conditional on living the law that is attached to that blessing. Some may feel that commandments and covenants are restrictive, limiting our ability to choose. Instead we should recognize obedience to law opens the door to the Lord being able to bless us.

> There is a law, irrevocably decreed in heaven before the foundations of this world, upon which all blessings are predicated—
>
> And when we obtain any blessing from God, it is by obedience to that law upon which it is predicated. (D&C 130: 20–21)

These verses are a great comfort because we know that by obeying a law, we will receive the blessing. Those blessing may not come in this life but they will come. As Elder Jeffrey R. Holland said: "Some blessings come soon, some come late, and some don't come until heaven; but for those who embrace the gospel of Jesus Christ, they come."[152]

If we are not living worthy of our promised blessings, we are actually just hurting ourselves. "He is left unto himself, to kick against the pricks" (D&C 121:38). I recently taught a young lady for whom I feel great concern. She is a beautiful girl that, at the present time, is not making good decisions. I don't know what her parents did to get her to come to seminary. Her body sat there but that is all. She absolutely refused to listen. She would sleep, try to listen to her music, or just be in her own world on the Internet. But she would not interact with me or the other members of the class. You could feel the resentment in her. Most people just tried to avoid her. I looked at this beautiful girl and I wanted to cry out, "why are you making your life so hard? How can you reject the support and love of the Lord? Life is hard! Don't live life on the outside of the gospel's safety net." The Lord is so very merciful that I know He is waiting for her to make an effort to reconcile her life with Him. I hope she does.

When we live the principles of the gospel, we can lay claim to blessings God has already promised to give us. President Hinckley challenged the Aaronic Priesthood holders in 2002 to live worthy to claim the blessing of angels in their lives.

> And so, to you young men who hold the Aaronic Priesthood, you have had conferred upon you that power which holds the keys to the ministering of angels. Think of that for a minute.
>
> You cannot afford to do anything that would place a curtain between you and the ministering of angels in your behalf.
>
> You cannot be immoral in any sense. You cannot be dishonest. You cannot cheat or lie. You cannot take the name of God in vain or use filthy language and still have the right to the ministering of angels.[153]

If we want to lay claim to the blessing of the ministering of angels, we need to live our lives according to the principles President Hinckley taught. I have lived much of my life with the hope that if I live worthy of a promised blessing, eventually that blessing will come. Life has not always gone the direction I planned. My life has been cluttered with unfulfilled expectations. Yet the Lord's promises are true and sure, and justice demands if I live the law associated with that blessing, the Lord will reward me with the appropriate blessings in His own due time. What great hope and comfort this principle brings to me.

As established earlier, one of the roles of an angel is to "*fulfil and to do the work of the covenants of the Father*, which he hath made unto the children of men" (Moroni 7:31). Angels may very well assist in our covenants being fully realized. Isn't it easier to face some of our trials if we believe that loved ones beyond the veil are cheering us on, giving us assistance, and even crying for us?

My mother-in-law died July 13, 1977. My husband and I were married January 23, 1976. Dave's mother had serious health difficulties, and my husband was an only child because of those health problems. His mother waited 27 years for him to marry and she was excited when we had our first child. She had always wanted additional children of her own. But eight months after our first child was born, Dave's mother died of a massive heart attack at the age of 60. We were devastated. As we added more children to our family, I would think, *Oh, I wish Pearl (my mother-in-law) was here to enjoy our children. She would have loved watching them grow.* One day, I was struggling with why she had to die so soon after we were married. Why couldn't she have been a part of our lives on earth for a longer time? Then I had the distinct impression that she was part of our lives and that she could bless our lives more from where she was after her death than if she had remained with us.

Since her death, my mother-in-law has been a part of our lives on several occasions. One Sunday when we were at church celebrating Mother's Day, I felt her presence so strongly that tears welled up in my eyes. I just knew she was there. I looked at my husband and said, "I think your mother is here today." He too felt her presence.

When our oldest daughter, Lisa, was born, I was shocked to see a family resemblance to Dave's departed mother. Her chin and hands are like her grandmother's. Lisa is very athletic, which is a talent that comes from Dave's mother. I have a very old picture of Pearl that hangs in an old oval picture frame. It hung for many years in the bedroom occupied by Lisa. One day, seven-year-old Lisa came to me with this question: "Mom, can you love someone you have never met?" Thinking I understood her intentions, I gave her a lecture about how love grows as we serve others and we find things that we have in common. When I finished what I thought was a brilliant answer, she simply said, "Oh, I was wondering because when I look at the picture in my room of Grandma Anthony, I love her." I humbly corrected myself, "Yes, you can love her, even though you don't know her, because I know how much she loves you."

Lisa herself has had some interesting interactions with her Grandma Anthony. I asked her to write down a few of these experiences:

"My dear grandmother passed away a year before I was born. Although I never met her while living on this earth, I have always felt a deep bond and connection with her. I remember many occasions in my life when the connection to my grandma was deeper than just a feeling but almost like she was physically holding me in her arms to comfort or protect me. My first profound connection happened when I was very young. I remember my parents receiving a couple of boxes of jewelry and personal items that had once belonged to my grandma. I cherished many of these items for years and still keep many of these objects tucked away in a safe place.

"I always loved hearing stories about my grandma, but along with the joy I felt when I would hear these stories, I also felt so much pain. I missed her so much it hurt and my heart broke knowing that she was gone. As a child I never understood why I felt so much pain for someone I had never even met. As time went on I began to realize the influence my grandma had in my life despite the fact that she was physically gone from this earth. I felt her love and guidance on many occasions. I also felt her disappointment and pain when I made wrong choices. Yet, through it all I knew she patiently stood by and never gave up on me. I am so thankful I was given this guardian angel.

"As a mother, I don't think it is possible to not worry about my children. I had a baby die shortly after birth (see chapter 1: Our Angel Gabe). I constantly pray that my son will be protected, cared for, and loved because I feel so helpless not being able to physically care for him. I don't have a day go by that I don't think about him and wonder if all is well. After spending some time at the cemetery one afternoon, I stood up to leave. I was walking toward my car when I suddenly realized I was not alone at that little headstone on my son's grave. I turned back toward the grave and even though I didn't see anyone standing there I knew my grandma was there. Without any hesitation I said, 'Take care of my son.' I heard her voice say, 'I will. I know what it feels like to not have your son.' The words that came to my mind were short and simple but the love behind her words was as deep as the love I felt for my child. I realized after she had said this to me that she had not been able to hold her son for years, that physically there was a barrier between her and her son. My father was an only child and it had been 31 years since my grandma had been on this earth to care for her child. I walked away that day knowing that my grandma loved my son and would care for him and watch over him while I was helpless to do so. I walked away seeing my dad in a new light; he was a son who had a mother that loved him unconditionally. The man that I had depended on for strength, protection, and guidance my whole life was also a child who would one day be in his mother's arms again."

I have *asked the Lord* to allow this grandmother to minister to my son that is not active in the Church. I may never know what labors she has performed, but I believe that she has been fully aware of my heartache and has assisted in any way she was permitted.

Every parent that has struggled with a wayward child will be touched with this beautiful story of comfort from beyond the veil. An anonymous mother from Utah wrote,

> One of my most precious experiences occurred when my wayward son had visited me and left me in tears once again. This child is like trying to hug a porcupine! He believes he is doing himself and everyone else a favor when he tells things "the way they are."
>
> That evening, I had been alone at home. Everyone in my support system was unavailable: my husband was away serving in a Church calling, my youngest son was at work, and my parents were out of town. I was completely defenseless when my son began to hurl unkind accusations and angry words.

> I remember the searing pain and agony I felt in the wake of his tirade. When he stomped out the door, I sank to the floor and sobbed. I felt myself spiraling into despair and loneliness. I thought that I had nowhere to run and nobody to turn to. As I wept uncontrollably, I realized that I wasn't alone; all I needed to do was talk to my Heavenly Father and ask for comfort.
>
> What occurred then was unexpectedly beautiful and priceless. As I poured out my agony and begged not to be alone, I asked for someone to come be with me and help me through this horrible time. Soon, I began to feel a warmth creep across my body. Immediately to my right, I sensed the presence of a grandfather to whom I had been particularly close in my youth. Then, to my left, I sensed the presence of my husband's grandmother, whom I had met only twice in our early marriage. She was sympathetic to my plight; she had lived her life without seeing any of her sons active in the Church. As these two family members stayed with me, I felt surrounded by love, peace, and the knowledge that families are connected in this life and the next.
>
> My husband and I have had many experiences with ancestors helping us, but this experience was especially sweet because it came to me in such a difficult moment. It was a vivid reminder that we are never alone. When we need help we will be ministered to by spirits who love us, know us, and want to help us succeed.[154]

Why would we choose to go through such difficult challenges alone? Living the gospel brings such comfort and when needed, hugs from beyond the veil. We can receive such peace. That is why it is difficult to understand why anyone would choose to not live the commandments and promises they have made with the Lord and risk forfeiting blessings from divine sources.

Elder Richard G. Scott explained how he drew strength in times of need from his wife who had preceded him in death by twenty years. "I didn't lose her. She's on the other side of the veil. We've been sealed in that holy ordinance of the temple and will be together forever. And at critical times in my life, when I need help, I can feel impressions come through the veil in such a way that I just thank Jeanene."[155]

Elder Scott was so sensitive and attuned to spiritual impressions that he recognized the help from his wife. If these blessings are not a part of our life, is it because of our own unbelief? Mormon confirmed that if angels have ceased to appear unto us it would be "because of unbelief" (Moroni 7:37). Mormon assures us that "so long as time shall last, or the earth shall stand, or there shall be one man upon the face thereof to be saved," there would be angels involved in our lives (Moroni 7:36).

Elder David L. Bednar stated,

> Parents who *honor temple covenants* are in a position to exert great spiritual influence over time on their children. Faithful members of the Church can find comfort in knowing that they can *lay claim to the promises of divine guidance and power*, through the inspiration of the Holy Ghost and the privileges of the priesthood, in their efforts to help family members receive the blessings of salvation and exaltation.
>
> The "tentacles of Divine Providence" . . . may be considered a type of spiritual power, a heavenly pull or tug that entices a wandering child to return to the fold eventually. Such an influence cannot override the moral agency of a child but nonetheless can invite and beckon.[156]

Elder Bednar stated that we could lay claim to the promises of divine guidance and power. Knowing that the Lord has already promised these blessings, why would we not have faith in and seek for this power in our lives and the lives of those we love so dearly? These blessing come not only to those who have wandered far from our reach but also to each and every member of our family. Which one of your family members would you not want to have the ministering of angels? President Joseph F. Smith teaches us that heavenly messengers are in our presence and that these heavenly messengers know us and they can see us.

> Surely those who have passed beyond, can see more clearly through the veil back here to us than it is possible for us to see to them from our sphere of action. I believe *we move and have our being in the presence of heavenly messengers and of heavenly beings*. We are not separate from them. We begin to realize, more and more fully, as we become acquainted with the principles of the gospel, as they have been revealed anew in this dispensation, that we are closely related to our kindred, to our ancestors, to our friends and associates and co-laborers who have preceded us into the spirit world. We cannot forget them; we do not cease to love them; we always hold them in our

> hearts, in memory, and thus we are associated and united to them by ties that we cannot break, that we cannot dissolve or free ourselves from. If this is the case with us in our finite condition, surrounded by our mortal weaknesses, short-sightedness, lack of inspiration and wisdom, from time to time, how much more certain it is and reasonable and consistent to believe that those who have been faithful, who have gone beyond and are still engaged in the work for the salvation of the souls of men, the opening of the prison doors to them that are bound, and proclaiming liberty to the captives, can *see us better than we can see them*; that they *know us better than we know them*.[157]

President Smith reminds us that the veil is very thin. We are recognized by the angels even though we don't recognize them. As members of The Church of Jesus Christ of Latter-day Saints, we may be living far beneath our privileges and passing up the blessings the Lord wants to grant us. One of those blessings may be the ministration of angels and the help they can give us throughout our lives. This Church holds the priesthood keys to the ministration of angels. Our Heavenly Father desires to bless us and give us the aid we need to maneuver through this life of tests, trials, and challenges. Some may go through life feeling alone and unloved when in reality there are angels surrounding us and we are just unaware. The fact that we are unaware does not change the reality that angels do exist and that without accepting and living for their assistance, we are living far below our divine blessings.

Angels are there in our defense. Elder Jeffrey R. Holland, as commissioner of the Church Educational System, said, "In the gospel of Jesus Christ you have help from both sides of the veil, and you must never forget that. When disappointment and discouragement strike—and they will—you remember and never forget that if our eyes could be opened we would see horses and chariots of fire as far as the eye can see riding at reckless speed to come to our protection. They will always be there, these armies of heaven, in defense of Abraham's seed."[158]

The blessing of angels is there for us. Being aware that they are there may open our eyes to recognize the help that is being offered.

President James E. Faust stated, "I would like to say a word about the ministering of angels. In ancient and modern times angels have appeared and given instruction, warnings, and direction, which benefited the people they visited. We do not consciously realize the extent to which ministering angels affect our lives. . . . Many of us feel that we have had this experience. Their ministry has been and is an important part of the gospel."[159]

We live in a very interesting time. President Hinckley said,

"We live in a season of war. We live in a season of arrogance. We live in a season of wickedness, pornography, immorality. All of the sins of Sodom and Gomorrah haunt our society."[160]

We also live in a time of the restoration of all things, where temples dot the earth, where the Book of Mormon is flooding the earth, and where righteous members are in every country. A time that has been anticipated by great prophets who were taught by angels of our day. "Our forefathers have awaited with anxious expectation to be revealed in the last times, which their minds were pointed to by the angels" (D&C 121:27).

I testify that angels are there. I do not ever expect to see an angel, but I have felt their influence. I am so grateful to know that if the situation warrants, they are not far from my side. This knowledge brings me peace. I feel so richly blessed to know that the Lord is orchestrating His plan not only for the world but also for my life. I feel so humbled to know that He is watching over me and knows my needs and administers to those needs through the Holy Ghost. One of his divine helps comes from angels. He knows when that divine help is given, how it is given, and what kind of help is given. God determines if and when angels will come. The older you get, the more loved ones you know personally on the other side veil. It is a testimony that families are eternal. Love never ceases. The purpose of this work is to seal us to those on the other side that are also invested in this labor.

I share the same testimony given by Sister Linda S. Reeves, second counselor in the Relief Society general presidency, when she said,

"I testify that as I have listened more intently and tried to exercise my faith, the Lord has been merciful to me and has helped make my burdens light. He has helped me to feel great peace about prayers that have not yet been answered. We bind the Lord to keep His promises when we keep our covenants and exercise our faith. Come to the temple . . . and *claim your blessings*!"[161]

Conclusion

Does acknowledging angels make us seem strange? Angels play an important part in our existence here. To deny them or shun the fact that we have access to their help beyond the veil seems to close the door on one of the guiding lights in our arsenal of divine directors.

Are we so confident that we don't need the help of angels to teach us how to combat life's challenges? Can we manage life so well that we don't need the warning and protection that angels are willing to give if directed by our Heavenly Father? When did we become so secure that we no longer need comfort? All these blessings await those that fall under the administration of the keys of the Aaronic Priesthood. Perhaps the only thing blocking us from receiving this special divine help is to acknowledge that angels can and do minister to us and then prepare our ears to hear and our hearts to feel. Elder Jeffrey R. Holland taught that we need to do just that. We need to testify of the reality of angels.

> May I suggest to you that one of the things we need to teach your students, and one of the things which will become more important in their lives the longer they live, is the reality of angels, their work, and their ministry. Obviously I speak here not alone of the angel Moroni, but also of those more personal ministering angels who are with us and around us, *empowered to help us*, and who do exactly that. . . .

> Perhaps more of us, including our students, could literally, or at least figuratively, behold the angels around us *if we would but awaken from our stupor and hear the voice of the Spirit as those angels try to speak*. . . . I believe we need to speak of and believe in and bear testimony to the ministry of angels more than we sometimes do. They constitute one of God's great methods of witnessing through the veil."[162]

What does he mean with the longer we live the more important angels ministry will be in our own personal lives? Perhaps the older we get the more we realize the blessings in our lives were influenced by angels. Maybe he means the more acquainted we become with the role of angels the more we see their influence. Maybe as we age we know more people that have passed to the other side. Maybe, as the world around us becomes increasingly wicked, our need for them will also be more evident.

Perhaps just becoming more aware of our own spiritual self will help us by becoming more aware of the spirits around us. President Harold B. Lee said if only our physical sense would sleep then we would be more aware of the angels.

> And if our eyes could be opened we could see those who have departed from us—a father, mother, brother, a sister, a child. We could see them, and sometimes when our physical senses are asleep, sometimes our spiritual self—and we have ears, spiritual ears, and spiritual eyes—sometimes they will be very keen and awake, and a departed one may come while we are lying asleep and come into our consciousness. We'll feel an impression. We'll wake up, where does it come from? It comes from the spirits of those whom we are sealed to.[163]

There have been times that I have felt their presence even though my eyes could not see them. Out of the blue you will feel someone near and in many cases even know who that person is. They are cheering for you. As Elder Dieter F. Uchtdorf said, "Even angels are cheering you on; they know of the great divine potential that lies within you."[164] I hope there are times in our lives when the veil will be thin and we will recognize this help and be aware of their care.

As the world around us deteriorates in greater and more wide spread wickedness, greater destruction and unrest, and greater devastation, our need of help from the other side of the veil will be more evident. How will we live in our modern-day Sodom and Gomorrah without divine help? I hope that this book will make us all aware that we are not alone in this battle for good.

Endnotes

1. Linda S. Reeves, "Claim the Blessings of Your Covenants," *Ensign*, November 2013, 119–20.

2. *New Testament: Student Study Guide* (Salt Lake, The Church of Jesus Christ of Latter-day Saints, 2003), 148; emphasis added. Angel comes from the Greek word *angelos* and the Hebrew *malak*. The term "angel" means "messenger."

3. Orson Pratt, *Journal of Discourses*, 17:148; emphasis added.

4. Mark L. McConkie, *Remembering Joseph* (Salt Lake City: Deseret Book, 2003), 210–11.

5. Mark L. McConkie, *Encyclopedia of Mormonism*, Harold B. Lee Library, Brigham Young University, Digital Publisher, Copyright 1992 Macmillan Publishing Company [Purchased by Gale Group in 1999]; Copyright 2001 Brigham Young University [copyright transferred to BYU in 2001] accessed November 12, 2015, http://eom.byu.edu/index.php/Translated_Beings.

6. Joseph Smith, *History of the Church*, 1839–1842, vol. 4 (Salt Lake City: Deseret Book, 1978), 425.

7. Joseph F. Smith, *Gospel Doctrine: Selections from the Sermons and Writings of Joseph F. Smith* (Salt Lake City: Deseret Book, 1968), 445, 456–57.

8. Jeffrey R. Holland, "The Ministry of Angels," *Ensign*, November 2008, 29–31; emphasis added.

9. *New Testament: Student Study Guide* (Salt Lake City: The Church of Jesus Christ of Latter-day Saints, 2003), 148; emphasis added.

10. Spencer W. Kimball, "Small Acts of Service," *Ensign*, December 1974.

11. William R. Walker, "Our Prophet Thomas S. Monson," CES Devotional for Young Adults, May 15, 2013 Brigham Young University–Idaho, accessed November 12, 2015, https://www.lds.org/broadcasts/article/ces-devotionals/2013/01/our-prophet-thomas-s-monson?lang=eng.

12. Thomas S. Monson, "We Never Walk Alone," *Ensign*, November 2013, 122–23.

13. Gabriel Middleton, "Stop Right Here," *New Era*, April 2005, 26–28.

14. Chieko N. Okazaki, "Raised in Hope," *Ensign*, November 1996, 89.

15. Jeffrey R. Holland, "The Ministry of Angels," *Ensign*, November 2008, 29–31; emphasis in original.

16. "As Sisters in Zion," *Hymns*, no. 309.

17. Russell M. Nelson, "Our Sacred Duty to Honor Women," *Ensign*, May 1999.

18. *History of Relief Society 1842–1966* (The General Board of Relief Society, 1966), 21; emphasis added.

19. Joy Webb Rigby, "Living by the Spirit," *Ensign*, August 1984, 15.

20. Dallin H. Oaks, "The Aaronic Priesthood and the Sacrament," *Ensign*, November 1998, 39.

21. Boyd K. Packer, "Personal Revelation, the Gift, the Test, and the Promise," *Ensign*, November 1994, 59.

22. Joseph Fielding Smith, *Teachings of the Prophet Joseph Smith* (Salt Lake City: Deseret Book, 1976), 325.

23. Donald W. Parry, "Angels, Chariots, and the Lord of Hosts," BYU Devotional 31 July 2012, accessed November 12, 2015, https://speeches.byu.edu/talks/donald-w-parry_angels-chariots-and-the-lord-of-hosts/.

24. Boyd K. Packer, *Mine Errand from the Lord, Selections from the Sermons and Writings of Boyd K. Packer*, ed. Clyde J. Williams (Salt Lake City: Deseret Book, 2008), 125.

25. Neal A. Maxwell, *Sermons Not Spoken* (Salt Lake City, Bookcraft, 1985), 21.

26. See Harold B. Lee, Conference Rerport October 1960, http://scriptures.byu.edu/.

27. Bruce C. Hafen, "When Do the Angels Come?" *Ensign*, April 1992, 12.

28. Joseph Smith, *Teachings of the Prophet Joseph Smith*, comp. Joseph Fielding Smith (Salt Lake City: Deseret Book, 1976), 326.

29. Joseph F. Smith, *Gospel Doctrine*, 5th ed. (Salt Lake City: Deseret Book, 1939), 436.

30. Daniel Peterson, "Life After Death is a Joyful fact, *Deseret News*, March 1, 2012, accessed November 12, 2015, http://www.deseretnews.com/article/765555334/Life-after-death-is-a-joyful-fact.html?pg=all.

31. Jeffrey R. Holland, *"However Long and Hard the Road"* (Salt Lake City: Deseret Book, 1985), 13–14; emphasis added.

32. "Dallin H. Oaks, "Joseph, the Man and the Prophet," *Ensign*, May 1996, 72.

33. Tad R. Callister, CES Devotional for Young Adults, January 12, 2014, Brigham Young University, accessed November 12, 2015, https://www.lds.org/broadcasts/article/ces-devotionals/2014/01/what-is-the-blueprint-of-christs-church?lang=eng.

34. Joseph Fielding Smith clarified that Gabriel was the great prophet Noah. "Joseph Smith revealed that Gabriel was Noah; Luke declared that it was the angel Gabriel who appeared to Zacharias and Mary"; Joseph Fielding Smith, *Answers to Gospel Questions*, vol. 3 (Salt Lake City: Deseret Book, 1979), 141.

35. In a very small way I have participated in a heavenly choir. I have witnessed the impact of hearing voices raised in praise to God. I attended the dedication of the Nauvoo temple, June 30, 2002, during the third session. We sat in the assembly hall on the very last row in front of the Tabernacle Choir. As the choir and the audience sang, "The Spirit of God," I was so overcome by emotion that I could hardly sing. The sound that I was hearing was not only coming from the choir and those around me but it seemed to come from the ceiling and the walls. I glanced at the ceiling several times for I was sure I would see a heavenly choir. There was not a dry eye in the audience. I can only imagine what the shepherds in Bethlehem felt that special night when the angels announced the birth of the Christ child.

Years later I was surprised to find an account of others hearing heavenly choirs at the Manti Temple dedication. This account was recorded in the Millennial Star. "On the 21st of May, before the opening exercises commenced, Brother A.C. Smyth, the chorister, seated himself at the organ, and rendered a piece of sacred music, a selection from Mendelssohn, at the conclusion of which, persons sitting near the center of the hall, and also on the stand at the west end, heard most heavenly voices and singing—it sounded to them most angelic, and appeared to be behind and above them, and they turned their heads in the direction of the sound, wondering if there was another choir in some other part of the Temple." "Spiritual Manifestations in the Manti Temple," *Millennial Star* 50 (1888): 521.

36. L. Tom Perry, "By the Hands of His Prophets," *Ensign*, August 1998, 49.

37. Joseph Smith, *Teachings of the Prophet Joseph Smith*, comp. Joseph Fielding Smith, 6th printing 1949 (Salt Lake City: Deseret News Press, 1938), 383.

38. David M. McConkie, "Teaching with the Power and Authority of God," *Ensign*, November 2013, 96.

39. Joseph Fielding McConkie, *Regional Studies in Latter-day Saint Church History: Illinois* (Provo, Utah: Brigham Young University, Department of Church History and Doctrine, 1995), 206–7.

40. Jeffrey R. Holland, "For a Wise Purpose," *Ensign*, January 1996, 12.

41. Mark E. Petersen, "The Angel Moroni Came," *Ensign*, November 1983; emphasis added.

42. Boyd K. Packer, "The Candle of the Lord," *Ensign*, January 1983.

43. Richard G. Scott, "Acquiring Spiritual Knowledge," *Ensign* November 1993, 86.

44. Joseph Fielding Smith, *Answers to Gospel Questions*, 5 vols. (Salt Lake City: Deseret Book, 1979), 2:151.

45. Joseph Fielding Smith, *Doctrines of Salvation Sermons and Writings of Joseph Fielding Smith*, 3 vols. comp. Bruce R. McConkie (Salt Lake City: Bookcraft, 1956), 1:48.

46. *Teachings of the Presidents of the Church: Wilford Woodruff* (Salt Lake City: The Church of Jesus Christ of Latter-day Saints), 49.

47. Oscar W. McConkie Jr., *Angels* (Salt Lake City: Deseret Book, 1975), 98–99.

48. As quoted in L. Tom Perry, "That Spirit Which Leadeth to Do Good," *Ensign*, May 1997.

49. Ibid.

50. Gordon B. Hinckley, *Teachings of Gordon B. Hinckley* (Salt Lake City: Deseret Book Company, 1997), 261.

51. Jeffrey R. Holland, "For a Wise Purpose," *Ensign*, January 1996, 12.

52. David A. Bednar, "Seek Learning by Faith," *Ensign*, September 2007.

53. "Q&A: Questions and Answers," *New Era*, April 1995.

54. Jeffrey R. Holland, "Place No More for the Enemy of My Soul," *Ensign*, May 2010; emphasis added.

55. Boyd K. Packer, "Cleansing the Inner Vessel," *Ensign*, November 2010, 76; emphasis added.

56. *Journal of Discourses*, 21:317.

57. Mark E. Petersen, "The Angel Moroni Came!," *Ensign*, November 1983.

58. Thomas S. Monson, "Hastening the Work," *Ensign*, June 2014.

59. Boyd K. Packer, *Mine Errand from the Lord: Selections from the Sermons and Writings of Boyd K. Packer*, ed. Clyde J. Williams (Salt Lake City: Deseret Book, 2008), 385.

60. Carol B. Thomas, "Developing Our Talent for Spirituality," *Ensign*, May 2001.

61. Accessed November 12, 2015, http://en.wikipedia.org/wiki/Touched_by_an_Angel.

62. L. Tom Perry, "The Priesthood of Aaron," *Ensign*, November 2010; emphasis added.

63. Dallin H. Oaks, "The Aaronic Priesthood and the Sacrament," *Ensign*, November 1998.

64. Ibid; emphasis added.

65. Neil L. Andersen, "Power in the Priesthood," *Ensign*, November 2013, 92.

66. Spencer J. Condie, "Becoming a Great Benefit to Our Fellow Beings," *Ensign*, May 2002, 44; emphasis in original.

67. Dallin H. Oaks, "The Aaronic Priesthood and the Sacrament," *Ensign*, November 1998, 37; emphasis added.

68. Boyd K. Packer, *Mine Errand from the Lord, Selections from the*

Sermons and Writing of Boyd K. Packer, ed. Clyde J. Williams (Salt Lake City: Deseret Book, 2008), 125.

69. Wilford Woodruff, *Discourses of Wilford Woodruff*, ed. G. Homer Durham (Salt Lake City: Bookcraft, 1990), 286, 300.

70. M. Russell Ballard, "Men and Women and Priesthood Power," *Ensign*, September 2014.

71. *Lectures on Faith*, 6:7

72. Carol B. Thomas, "Sacrifice: An Eternal Investment," *Ensign*, May 2001, 64.

73. Hugh Nibley, *Of All Things* (Salt Lake City: Signature Books, 1981), 42.

74. Lucy Mack Smith, *History of Joseph Smith By His Mother*, notes and comments by Preston Nibley (Salt Lake City: Stevens and Wallis, 1945), 83.

75. Jacob F. Gates, "Testimony of Jacob Gates," *Improvement Era*, March 1912, 92.

76. *Teachings of Presidents of the Church: Joseph Smith* (Salt Lake City: The Church of Jesus Christ of Latter-day Saints, 2007), 419.

77. William Hurst, *Diary of Frederick William Hurst*, comp. Samuel H. and Ida Hurst (1961), 204.

78. Joseph Fielding Smith, *Doctrines of Salvation Sermons and Writings of Joseph Fielding Smith*, 3 vols. comp. Bruce R. McConkie (Salt Lake City: Bookcraft, 1956), 1:196.

79. Dieter F. Uchtdorf, "Are You Sleeping through the Restoration?," *Ensign*, May 2014, 59.

80. Henry B. Eyring, "Raising Expectations," August 4, 2004 CES Satellite Training Broadcast, accessed November 12, 2015, http://broadcast.lds.org/si/training-broadcast/2004-08-04-eyring-raising-expectations-32k-eng.mp3.

81. Quentin L. Cook, "Roots and Branches," *Ensign*, May 2014, 46–47; emphasis added.

82. Boyd K. Packer, *Mine Errand from the Lord Selections from the Sermons and Writings of Boyd K. Packer*, ed. Clyde J. Williams (Salt Lake City: Deseret Book, 2008), 128.

83. Russell M. Nelson, "Generations Linked in Love," *Ensign*, May 2010.

84. Quentin L. Cook, "Roots and Branches," *Ensign*, May 2014, 46.

85. Merle Lester, "A Visit From Milton," *Ensign*, April 2014, 70, 72.

86. Wilford Woodruff, *Journal of Discourses*, 19:229, or Classic Stories from the Lives of Our Prophets comp. Leon R. Hartshorn (Salt Lake City: Deseret Book, 1971), 126–27.

87. Heber J. Grant, "Comforting Manifestations": Excerpts from Funeral Sermon, *Improvement Era*, February 1931.

88. *Our Heritage: A Brief History of The Church of Jesus Christ of Latter-day Saints* (Salt Lake City: The Church of Jesus Christ of Latter-day Saints, 1996), 99.

89. Gordon B. Hinckley, "Living in the Fulness of Times," *Ensign*, November 2001.

90. Donald W. Parry, "Angels, Chariots, and the Lord of Hosts," BYU Devotional 31, July 2012. https://speeches.byu.edu/talks/donald-w-parry_angels-chariots-and-the-lord-of-hosts/.

91. Linda S. Reeves, "Worthy of Our Promised Blessings," *Ensign*, November 2015.

92. Mark E. Petersen, "The Angel Moroni Came," *Ensign*, November 1983.

93. Brian H. Stuy, ed., *Collected Discourses*, 3 vols., June 25, 1893.

94. Ibid.

95. Orson F. Whitney, *The Life of Heber C. Kimball* (Published by

The Kimball Family, Salt Lake City, Utah, Printed at the Juvenile Instructor Office, 1888), 43–44.

96. *Church History in the Fulness of Times, Student Manual*, Religion 341–24 (Salt Lake City: The Church of Jesus Christ of Latter-day Saints, 2003), 57.

97. Bruce C. Hafen, "When Do the Angels Come?," *Ensign*, April 1992.

98. James E. Faust, "Refined in Our Trials," *Ensign*, February 2006, 2–7.

99. John A. Widtsoe, *Evidences and Reconciliations* (Salt Lake City: Bookcraft, 1995), 402–3.

100. Ibid.

101. Larry E. Dahl, "I Have a Question," *Ensign*, March 1988.

102. Ibid.

103. Bruce R. McConkie, *Mormon Doctrine* (Salt Lake City: Bookcraft, 1966), 341–42.

104. Dallin H. Oaks, "Bible Stories and Personal Protection," *Ensign*, November 1992.

105. Ibid.

106. Ronald A. Rasband, "The Joyful Burden of Discipleship," *Ensign*, May 2014, 10–11.

107. Crystal Simmons, "Spring Shoorting: Community Remembers Stay Family," Cypress Creek Mirror, accessed May 1, 2016, http://www.yourhoustonnews.com/cypresscreek/news/spring-shooting-community-remembers-stay-family/article_a8b3a860-0a5a-11e4-be0c-0019bb2963f4.html.

108. Jeffrey R. Holland, "Place No More For the Enemy of My Soul," *Ensign*, May 2010; emphasis added.

109. Boyd K. Packer, "Cleansing the Inner Vessel," *Ensign*, November 2010; emphasis added.

110. Dallin H. Oaks, "Balancing Truth and Tolerance," *Ensign*, February 2013; emphasis added.

111. David A. Bednar, "The Hearts of the Children Shall Turn," *Ensign*, November 2011; emphasis added.

112. As quoted in Boyd K. Packer, *The Holy Temple* (Salt Lake City: Bookcraft, 1991), 252.

113. As quoted in Richard G. Scott, "How to Obtain Revelation and Inspiration for Your Personal Life," *Ensign*, May 2012.

114. Harold B. Lee, *Teachings of Harold B. Lee*, ed. Clyde J. Williams (Salt Lake City: Bookcraft, 1998), 614.

115. Joseph Fielding Smith, "Funeral Services for Elder Richard L. Evans," *Ensign*, December 1971.

116. Pat Reavy, "Timpview Sophmore Dies One Week After Reportedly Getting the Flu," *Deseret News*, February 2, 2013, accessed November 12, 2015, http://www.deseretnews.com/article/865572140/Timpview-sophomore-dies-one-week-after-reportedly-getting-flu.html?pg=all.

117. Heber C. Kimball, *Journal of Discourses*, 3:230.

118. Ibid., 10:246.

119. *Classic Stories from the Lives of Our Prophets*, comp. Leon R. Hartshorn (Salt Lake City: Deseret Book, 1988), 57.

120. *Autobiography of Parley Parker Pratt* (Salt Lake City: Deseret Book, 1938), 114–15.

121. Harold B. Lee, *Stand Ye in Holy Places* (Salt Lake City: Deseret Book, 1974), 139; emphasis added.

122. "Praise to the Man," *Hymns*, no. 27.

123. Harold B. Lee, *The Teachings of Harold B. Lee*, ed. Clyde J. Williams (Salt Lake City: Bookcraft, 1996), 614.

124. "Count Your Blessings," *Hymns*, no. 241.

125. Accessed November 15, 2015, http://en.wikipedia.org/wiki/File:Carl_Heinrich_Bloch_-_Gethsemane.jpg.

126. Bruce R. McConkie, *The Mortal Messiah: From Bethlehem to Calvary*, vol. 4 (Salt Lake City: Deseret Book, 1981), 4:125.

127. Jeffrey R. Holland, "The Ministry of Angels," *Ensign*, November 2008.

128. Andrew Jenson, *LDS Biographical Encyclopedia*, vol. 1 (Salt Lake City: Deseret News Press, 1901–36), 283.

129. Hyrum L. Andrus, *Joseph Smith the Man and the Seer* (Salt Lake City: Deseret Book, 1961), 128–29.

130. *Teachings of Presidents of The Church: Harold B. Lee* (Salt Lake City: The Church of Jesus Christ of Latter-day Saints, 2000), 182–83; emphasis added.

131. Marvin J. Ashton, "There Are Many Gifts," *Ensign*, November 1987, 20.

132. Michael R. Morris, "Sherrie's Shield of Faith," *Ensign*, June 1995.

133. Jeffrey R. Holland, "The Ministry of Angels," *Ensign*, November 2008.

134. Robert D. Hales, "The Covenant of Baptism: To Be in the Kingdom and of the Kingdom," *Ensign*, November 2000, 6.

135. Harold B. Lee, The Teaching of Harold B. Lee, ed. Clyde J. Williams (Salt Lake City: Bookcraft, 1996), 59–60; emphasis added.

136. Harold B. Lee, "Stand Ye in Holy Places," *Ensign*, July 1973.

137. Wilford Woodruff, The Discourses of Wilford Woodruff, ed. G. Homer Durham (Salt Lake City: Bookcraft, 1990), 229–31; emphasis added.

138. *Journal of Discourses*, 15:127.

139. N. Eldon Tanner, "Are You Taking Your Priesthood for

Granted?" *Ensign*, May 1976, 41; emphasis added.

140. *Journal of Discourses*, 8:257; emphasis added.

141. *Discourse of Brigham Young*, arranged by John A. Widtsoe (Salt Lake City: Deseret Book, 1954), 69.

142. (Christian Religious Writings/Bible) New Testament the destroyer, a name given to the Devil (Revelation 9:11) [via Late Latin from Greek, from apollunai to destroy totally], accessed November 12, 2015, http://www.thefreedictionary.com/Apollyon] [n. (ȧ*băd''dŬn) [Heb. *ābaddōn* destruction, abyss, fr. *ābad* to be lost, to perish.] 1. The destroyer, or angel of the bottomless pit;—the same as Apollyon and Asmodeus. 2. Hell; the bottomless pit, accessed November 12, 2015, http://biblehub.com/topical/a/abaddon.htm.

143. Harold B. Lee, *The Teachings of Harold B. Lee*, ed. Clyde J. Williams (Salt Lake City: Bookcraft, 1996), 32–33.

144. *Teachings of the Prophet Joseph Smith*, selected and arranged by Joseph Fielding Smith (Salt Lake City: Deseret News Press, 6th printing 1945), 181; emphasis added.

145. Lucy Mack Smith, *History of Joseph Smith by His Mother*, ed. Preston Nibley (Salt Lake City: Stevens and Wallis, 1945), 81.

146. Spencer W. Kimball, *The Miracle of Forgiveness* (Salt Lake City: Bookcraft, 1969), 117.

147. Boyd K. Packer, "The Holy Temple," *Ensign*, Feb. 1995, 36.

148. *Journal of Discourses*, 3:205–6.

149. *Teachings of the Prophet Joseph Smith*, selected and arranged by Joseph Fielding Smith (Salt Lake City: Deseret News Press, 6th printing 1945), 226.

150. Boyd K. Packer, "Personal Revelation: The Gift, the Test, and the Promise," *Ensign*, November 1994, 61; emphasis in original.

151. James E. Faust, "The Great Imitator" *Ensign*, November 1987.

152. Jeffrey R. Holland, "An High Priest of Good Things to Come," *Ensign*, November 1999.

153. Gordon B. Hinckley, "Personal Worthiness to Exercise the Priesthood," *Ensign*, May 2002, 52.

154. Larry Barkdull, "Angels Will Come," *Meridian Magazine*, February 9, 2011.

155. Church News, *Deseret News*, "Scientist Forsook Career," September 27, 2015, 3.

156. David A. Bednar, "Faithful Parents and Wayward Children, Sustaining Hope While Overcoming Misunderstanding," *Ensign*, March 2014; emphasis added.

157. Joseph F. Smith, "In the Presence of the Divine," Conference address given April 1916; emphasis added. http://emp.byui.edu /satterfieldb/quotes/Spirit%20World/Veil%20is%20Thin.html.

158. Jeffrey R. Holland, "For Times of Trouble", BYU Devotional, March 8, 1980, speeches.byu.edu.

159. James E. Faust, "A Royal Priesthood," *Ensign*, May 2006.

160. Gordon B. Hinckley, "Living in the Fulness of Times," *Ensign*, November 2001.

161. Linda S. Reeves, "Claim the Blessings of Your Covenants," *Ensign*, November 2013, 120; emphasis added.

162. Jeffry R. Holland, "A Standard unto My People," (address to religious educators at a symposium on the Book of Mormon), Brigham Young University, August 9, 1994, 11–13; emphasis added.

163. *The Teachings of Harold B. Lee*, ed. Clyde J. Williams (Salt Lake City: Bookcraft, 1998), 58.

164. Dieter F. Uchtdorf, "The Wind Beneath Your Wings," BYU Devotional November 11, 2003, accessed November 12, 2015, https:// speeches.byu.edu/talks/dieter-f-uchtdorf_wind-beneath-wings/.

About the Author

Sherrie Anthony was born and raised in Salt Lake City. She entered the mission home two hours late because she was marching in her graduation ceremony from the University of Utah with a Bachelor of Science degree. In December 1975, she completed a mission to the Hawaii Honolulu Mission and, seven weeks later, married her best friend who had "progressed" while waiting for her to serve a mission. When the youngest of their five child turned eighteen, Sherrie pursued a desire to teach seminary. That desire had been placed in her heart when she taught early morning seminary as a newlywed for a short time in Houston, Texas. The process to become a full-time teacher was grueling, but the Lord opened doors that previously had been shut and she was hired. After teaching twelve years, she and her husband retired and are currently serving as full-time CES missionaries in the Washington, DC, North Mission. Sherrie and Dave are the grandparents of sixteen grandchildren.

0 26575 18717 5